Nature and Its Inhabitants

Book One

THE DISOBEDIENT OWL

and Other Tales

CARL EWALD

Translation and Adaptations
William V. Zucker

Illustrations
Subhadeep Ghosh

Available in these formats:
978-7357216-0-6 (Paperback)
978-7357216-1-3 (eBook)

Library of Congress Control Number: 2020917933

Editing: Graham W. Schofield

Cover Design/Illustrations: Subhadeep Ghosh

Published by the translator.
Forgeus Press / Tucson, Arizona 85716 U.S.A.
Phone: 520-327-0192

www.classicnaturestoriesforkids.com

williamzucker@msn.com

Other Translations by William V. Zucker

The Orphaned Ducklings / Book Two
Carl Ewald

The Unfortunate Carp! / Book Three
Carl Ewald

The Invincible Sea / Book Four
(Coming 2021)
Carl Ewald

Five Children's Stories /A Learning Guide
(Coming 2021)
Carl Ewald & William V. Zucker

The Children's Crusade: A Synopsis /
Carl Ewald

Danish Fairy Tales & Rhymes /
Anna S. Seidelin

To my brother Sandy and to June D. for setting me on the path.

To Andreas, Rolf, Kristopher, Bodil, Erling, Marion, and Edith for keeping me on the journey.

Mange tak allesammen.

Translator's Introduction...

Along with the need to entertain, parents, teachers, librarians and all who appreciate quality reading for children will see the value in providing them with stories offering a penetrating glimpse of the natural world and its many creatures, plant and animal, unadorned by the 'fluff' so typical of children's stories today.

The highly acclaimed author of these stories, Carl Ewald (1856-1908), wrote them in Denmark over 100 years ago. His early training as a field biologist and forester gave him huge insights into nature and spurred an interest that lasted throughout his life.

These amazing stories are as valid today as they were in his time, and they offer so much to a new generation of children throughout the English-speaking world. They inform, they teach, and they stimulate the imagination.

The majority of Ewald's stories remain untranslated into English, but not all, and thus I am not the first to take on this task. However, my versions adapted from the original Danish are intended to be the most modern and relevant to children in the 21st Century.

While technically and visually fascinating to look at, nature is not what the Disney films typically portray, which is unfortunate. It misleads children—and adults!—giving them an incorrect and distorted understanding of how nature really works.

Charles Darwin, with his theory of evolution through natural selection, was a near contemporary of the author. He informed and enthused Ewald who quickly embraced these ideas in his writings for children and penned twenty collections of nature stories. They take place in woods, in lakes, in streams, in the ocean, in fields, in bogs and swamps, in jungles, and even out in space.

Unlike other writers of fables that came before him, it did not satisfy Carl Ewald merely to allow his animals and plants—or even something as mundane as the wind—to talk and act like people. His major concern was to steer children (and their mentors) into learning the unvanished truth of nature's amazing complexity, while attempting to make it simple enough for a child to understand.

In summary, he knew his natural history and explained it in fable form. He didn't sentimentalize nature either; he knew it too well. He knew the stronger win out, and that they bear no feelings for the weaker; for Ewald, there was no sense talking morality to the fox bent on raiding the ranger's hen house.

Darwin's principles became the inspiration for Ewald's stories, which reveal an often harsh life, complicated by a web of species interrelations. Some may argue this approach is perhaps not appropriate for children, but others—especially with today's appeal for transparency in all matters—can equally stress to the contrary that faithful-to-nature stories are preferable.

This first book of ten stories is a sampling of not just the sweep of Ewald's interest in revealing a real-world nature, but also the high literary quality of his stories. There are many more stories, and I can hardly wait to bring them all to you.

My grateful thanks to Erling and Lis Pilgaard for help with translation chores. For invaluable guidance and help with the text, I thank Graham Schofield, and to Subhadeep Ghosh, my sincerest gratitude for his outstanding illustrations and book cover design, but especially for his patience and appreciation of how text and visuals need to coalesce.

William V. Zucker
Tucson, Arizona - U.S.A.
2021

When you finish reading this book... would you please write a review!

Authors (and translators) love hearing from their readers.

To help other readers and children find these realistic descriptions of nature by Carl Ewald, please let the translator know what you thought about the stories in this book.

Please leave an honest review on Amazon or Goodreads or your other preferred online store.

(If you are under 14, please ask a grown-up to help you).

Thank you!

P.S. Please mention what your favorite story was.

www.amazon.com

Choose your story...

Don't Mess With Lady Spider

Chapter 1

Trees and bushes once crowded the fence row, but now they were all cut down, and only long, thin twigs emerged from the stumps. But in between, wild carrot and wild parsley were growing along with other similar plants that all looked alike. Those who knew no better would call them weeds.

Their stems were almost as long as the branches of the bushes had been, which made them think they were just as important as real bushes that didn't wither in the fall and, like a daisy or a pansy, didn't have to begin again from a little seed. They bulged and bristled, tossing in the wind until they toppled. They dropped their leaves and got new ones as though time didn't matter, but if anyone asked what they were all up to, they made light of it or denied it.

Their lovely white flowers rose up into the air like umbrellas, while the stick-thin branches growing out from the stumps resembled nothing more than overgrown, scrawny kids, unable to produce flowers or fruit.

"This is like a whole forest," said the mouse late one evening as she sat under the canopy of white and deep green flora, peeking up with her bright eyes.

"We are the forest," said the wild carrot haughtily.

"Please look around," added the wild parsley. "If you find it cozy here, build your nest among us. Use whatever we have."

"Oh, don't get involved with them," urged the nearest stump twig. "They brag in the summer, but in the fall, they wither, and 'poof', they're gone."

"I know nothing about the fall," said the wild parsley.

"I don't believe in fall," said the wild carrot. "It's just a silly joke they tell little bushes."

"But it's true about fall," said the mouse, "and then comes winter, so, it's a good idea to have enough food until spring. In fact, that reminds me, I need to dig a little hole among the stumps and stones and store up provisions."

"Dig in the ground if you like and..." began the wild parsley.

"We aim for higher things," interrupted the wild carrot with a sneer.

They looked around a while, saying nothing until the wild parsley sighed and said aloud what both were thinking.

“If only we were strong enough that a bird would come and build its nest among our leaves.”

“We could shade it, and it would feel so relaxed with us that the stump twigs would die of envy,” said the wild carrot.

“How about taking me?” inquired a voice.

They quickly took a look around and saw an unusul, quite strange-looking, and creeping gray and black creature which had come strolling by on the fence.

“Who are you?” asked the wild parsley.

“My proud name is spider,” said the intruder.

“Can you fly?” asked the wild carrot.

“I can do a little of everything when it’s necessary.”

"Do you eat flies?" asked the wild parsley.

"All day long."

"Do you lay eggs?" asked the wild carrot. "You are a female, aren't you? You sound like one."

"Yes, thank heavens," said the spider.

"In that case, you're as welcome as the birds are," said the wild parsley.

"Oh yes, we're thrilled to have you," added the wild carrot. "You look light, and so you won't break our stems."

"Just build whenever you want to," said the wild parsley. "There's plenty of material here along the row. It won't make the slightest difference if you pinch a leaf or two here and there."

"Thanks, but I brought my own materials with me," said the spider.

"I don't see any baggage," said the wild carrot.

"Possibly your mate is bringing it along?" inquired the wild parsley.

"Heavens, I don't have a mate," retorted the spider and shook a little as if the idea disturbed her.

"Oh, you poor thing," said the mouse, joining the conversation. "That must make you feel awfully sad."

"What nonsense!" argued the spider. "Such girlish silliness makes us females such laughable and contemptible creatures. You always say, 'my mate... this,' and 'my mate... that.' What good are males for, anyway? Just a lot of ridiculous trouble if you ask me. If I ever take a mate, he doesn't stand a chance of living with me!"

"My, how you talk!" said the mouse. "I can't think of anything worse than living without my mate. How could I manage the kids without his help, the dear soul?"

"Oh, stop it! Such nonsense about kids," argued the spider. "I don't understand where all this soppy thinking comes from. Just lay your eggs in the right place and let the newborns take care of themselves."

"She doesn't sound at all like a regular bird," said the wild parsley suspiciously.

"She scares me a little," admitted the wild carrot.

"Say what you like," said the spider, "but I rarely associate with birds. If there are too many birds, I wouldn't stay around here."

"Oh dear," said the wild parsley, now fearing that the spider was about to leave. "No one ever comes here anymore."

"When they chopped all the trees and bushes down," said the wild carrot, "all the birds fled into the woods."

"Yes, it's lonely here," said the stump twig sadly. "You never hear a sound."

"Well, I think it looks nice here," said the spider. "With all these flies buzzing around, I'm sure I'll be content."

"Well, here we are when you're ready," offered the wild carrot and the wild parsley straightening up and trying to look inviting.

Chapter 2

As the spider crawled down to the ground and looked around, the mouse and the stems of wild carrot and wild parsley watched carefully.

"Pardon me," said the mouse. "Why do you bother building a nest if you let your eggs look after themselves?"

"Look, you annoying creature," sighed the spider, turning around to face the mouse. "I'm an independent female. I'm only interested in taking care of myself and what is mine. If I ever stoop so low as to pick a mate, let the little nothing take care of himself."

"Little nothing?" questioned the mouse, her eyes opening wide. "My mate is larger and stronger than I am."

"Well, I don't know him," said the spider dismissively. "But I'm four times bigger than the males I know, all useless specimens and not worth as much as a fly. Who wants to live with them? Anyway, just leave me alone because I have to build a new place to live."

"You'd better wait until it gets light," said the wild parsley.

"What are you going to build with?" asked the wild carrot.

"I like the dark," said the spider, before adding impatiently, "and I said already, I always carry my building material with me."

With that, she climbed up to the top of the wild carrot and surveyed the landscape. In the fading light, the wild parsley looked on enviously.

"You'll need a good pair of eyes to see anything at night," said the mouse. "Mine aren't that good except for seeing the cat that ventures over from the farm. I wouldn't want to build my nest without better lighting."

"I have eight eyes," replied the spider arrogantly, "and they see plenty. And eight legs too, so I can take care of myself where and when necessary. There's no fuss and nonsense with me."

With that, she pushed her back against wild carrot's stem she was sitting on and plunged headfirst into the air.

"She'll break her neck," screamed the mouse, quite terrified.

"I have no neck," sniffed the spider, now clinging upside down to the underside of one of wild parsley's leaves. "And if I had one, I wouldn't break it. Go home to your darling mate and cuddle him, and when you come back tomorrow, you'll see what a real female can do on her own when she doesn't waste her time with all that lovey-dovey stuff."

Somewhat offended, the mouse muttered that she'd better feed the family and scurried off into the darkness. Had she stayed, she might never have had a wink of sleep because the spider was behaving so strangely.

She jumped headfirst into the air, from leaf to leaf and stem to stem, never making a single mistake, or hurting herself in the slightest. Sometimes she climbed up and then, even though she had no wings, she descended slowly again. Back and forth, up and down, she worked the whole night.

"She is a bird," twittered the wild parsley happily.

"Of course she is," sneered the wild carrot. "What else could she be?"

But the tree stump twigs flapped scornfully at one another.

"Nonsense! She's not a bird," the nearest one argued. "Can she sing? Have you heard so much as a peep from her? Birds used to sing in our branches all the time before they chopped us down."

Puzzled by the question, wild carrot and wild parsley looked suspiciously at each other. When the spider rested for a moment to catch her breath, wild parsley posed a question.

"Can you sing?"

"That's ridiculous," said the spider. "Do you think I'd bother myself with such nonsense? What's worth singing about? Life is just sweat and tears. If a single female will make it, she has to get on with life and work."

"Birds sing," said the wild carrot.

"Well, you don't," asserted the spider, before adding, "They sing because they're in love and I'm not. Why should I waste time singing?"

"Wait until the right one comes along," said the wild parsley dreamily as the wild carrot looked a little hurt.

"If any male shows up here, he had better watch out!" said the spider.

Then she went back to jumping into the air headfirst.

When the dawn broke, the wild carrot and wild parsley were astounded.

The spider was hanging in the middle of the air between their stems. She was curled up with her legs close to her belly and was sleeping like a baby.

"Is she sitting on you?" asked the wild carrot.

"Not that I can feel," retorted the wild carrot, then sounding not so certain asked, "Isn't she sitting on you?"

"No, she isn't," replied the wild parsley.

"She isn't sitting on us either," said the stump twig.

"Then she must be a bird," said the wild parsley and wild carrot excitedly.

"But a bird doesn't hang in the middle of the air sleeping," argued the stump twigs.

"She's a witch," said the mouse that had suddenly appeared again. "Just wait until it gets properly light, and we'll see for ourselves."

Chapter 3

When the sun was up, they saw it. Between the leaves and stems of the wild carrot and wild parsley stretched a beautiful pattern of fine threads, crisscrossing each other and glimmering in the sunshine. Other threads made circles inside circles. It was a true delight to see, but the spider was no longer there.

"Oh," said the mouse. "Now I understand about where she would live, but where is she? She was sitting right there in the center, but now she's gone."

"I'm here, you silly mouse," said the spider from underneath a leaf. "I don't like the bright sunshine. What do you think of my work so far?"

"Well..." said the mouse, "actually, I think it's a very odd nest."

"Nest?" squeaked the spider as she stuck her head out to peer down at the mouse. "What are you talking about? You assume I'm just a weak, pitiful female like you. What do I need a nest for? It's just fine underneath this leaf where it is shady and comfortable. The threads are my web which I use to snare flies. I don't go looking for food—I let it come to me!"

While the plants and the mouse considered this latest piece of information, the spider came out from under the leaf and looked to the sky.

"I think if it will rain soon, I'd better finish my work," she said and jumped back onto her web.

A while later, the sun disappeared behind the clouds. It rained quietly, and when it stopped, the spider came out, stretching her eight legs into the humid air with delight.

And then she went back to work.

In silent awe, they all watched her draw several fine threads, all at the same time, out of her belly. Then she combed them out with the tips of her legs, twisting them together until they formed a single heavy thread before she hung them where she thought the web had too big an opening or looked too weak. As the sun peeked from behind a cloud once more, the mouse came back out and now marveled at the web. Raindrops were clinging to the threads, and she realized they were sticky so caught flies couldn't move in them. It was so beautiful, and they all admired it.

"I've simply done what I need to... in order to eat," explained the spider.

Just then, a starling showed up and sat on top of one of the long branches.

“Isn’t there a snack around here?” he said. “Something tasty like a nice fat larva or a spider?”

The wild carrot and wild parsley didn’t say a thing, terrified at losing their tenant. The mouse crept back into her hole, but the stump twig gave the game away and shouted that a delicious, fat spider had arrived the day before and spun its web in the night. The starling had a good look around, but then with a terse ‘I see nothing,’ it flew off again. So where was the spider? They were all puzzled.

Before the bird had even landed, quick as lightning, the spider had lowered herself down to the ground on a long thin thread and lay there among the clumps of soil as though she were dead. Now she crawled back up again, positioning herself in the center of the web with all eight legs stretched out.

“That was close,” she said, “but now it’s my turn.”

While the starling’s brief visit had distracted everyone, a nice little fly had come by and, not noticing the web, flew right into it, got caught and became all tangled up.

“That’s a start,” said the spider, and she bit the fly with her outer jaws full of poison; the fly died immediately. Then she ate it, as she did with the next three that flew into her web, and then she was full.

As the day wore on, and the plants tossed their heads in the breeze to cool down, and the mouse and the spider snoozed. Several miserable-looking small flies got caught in the web, but she left them hanging and squirming, not wanting even to touch them. But when a ripe, fat fly came by, she woke up and gave it a nasty bite, spun a little net around it, and hung it up on the side of her web.

“I’ll save you for later when I’m hungry, and there isn’t much to eat,” she said.

“That’s sensible,” said the mouse, finally agreeing. “But, how you hunt for food is far too tricky for me. Using poison just like a snake is a dirty trick.”

“Do you think so?” responded the spider scornfully with her nose in the air. “Is it any worse than what the rest of you do? Do you blow a trumpet to warn your prey, you sneak? You little goody-two-shoes mouse.”

“I gather nuts and acorns, and whatever else turns up, and I’ve never hurt anyone!” squeaked the mouse. “I’m not a robber or a murderer like you, thank heavens!”

“You’re such a sweet, little, old-fashioned prissy,” said the spider. “You’re happy with what falls in front of you. Then you go home and allow your kids and your mate to cuddle you. That’s not for me; I’m made of sterner stuff. But I have an appetite; I want meat—delicious, juicy fly meat—and lots of it. I ask for nothing but take what I need. That way, I have all the glorious pleasure to myself; if it doesn’t go my way, I don’t go around whining. It would be a better world if more females were like me.”

“You’re so common,” said the mouse.

“Nonsense,” replied the spider. “Six of one, half a dozen of the other, and I’m not worse than anybody else. The wild carrot and wild parsley fight over the butterflies and the bees. They steal light and space from each other."

"That's right," agreed the wild parsley.

"Crazy female," muttered the wild carrot, not wanting to admit the truth.

"You get so sentimental about these 'poor flies' that I capture, but that's my food," asserted the spider. "The farmer would kill a fly in a second just because it buzzed in his face. Tit for tat. You're just so full of the touchy-feely stuff."

The mouse looked like she wanted to argue, but the spider quickly jumped in again.

"Incidentally, I wouldn't mind changing my name at all. You can call me the Spinner if you like. A cute little female like you can probably tolerate that. It suits me fine too, because there's not an animal in the world that spins as beautifully as me."

"That may be true," said the mouse shaking her head, "but your business is awful, and you are not nice to look at."

"So, that's your problem," responded the spider laughing. "Now look, Little Mousey, my plain gray dress suits me; I'm not looking for attention. Thank heavens I don't have to dress up in some fancy fur, like other strutting and panting females looking for some easy loving. It's enough to make any sensible creature feel ashamed. But these hussies feel contempt for me because of my simple dress. Let them. I couldn't care less about them... and I'll eat anything that ventures into my web."

Once more, the mouse shook her head, but this time she said nothing, turned around, and left. As she disappeared from sight, the wild parsley and wild carrot whispered to each other as the spider crouched in her web, legs extended, digesting the fly she'd caught earlier.

Chapter 4

Later that day, when the sun was hot, the mouse returned to the shade beneath the plants and peered up, looking for the spider.

"Is she sleeping?" asked the mouse.

"I think so," said the wild parsley, "and I'd be careful not to wake her up with your chatter."

"She is our very own bird," said the wild carrot proudly. "Even though she may not act like the other birds, she has done us the honor to build her home here in safety, and so we insist she deserves everyone's respect."

"Some bird!" scoffed the stump twig.

"She's better than nothing," retorted the wild parsley before the wild carrot could.

"Toothpicks like you should just shut up," added the wild carrot. "No one will build anything in you."

"She's not a bird," said the mouse, "but she can still be good to have around. I think she's poor and unhappy and, despite her denials, getting desperate. Maybe her lover cheated on her; that can hurt. My first mate ran away with a white mouse just as I was giving birth to the kids, so I'm speaking from experience."

"That's neither here nor there," said the wild parsley thoughtfully, "but what are we going to do about her?"

"We have to make her happy," suggested the mouse. "If she lives such a lonely life, she'll get more depressed each day until she snuffs out every gentle feeling in her. If only we could find her a mate."

"Yes—if only we could," said the wild parsley dreamily.

"Then maybe she'd build a real nest with small eggs inside," said the wild carrot, warming to the idea.

"Maybe she'd sing to her kids," said the wild parsley, forgetting the spider's previous views on the matter.

"Then we'd be just as elegant as the bushes once were," said the wild carrot.

"What are you all going on about now?" asked the spider, sticking her head out from under the leaf.

"We're talking about you," said the mouse. "We think you need a mate. In the long run, it's not good for a female to be single. You'll get strange and become bitter. You don't know how wonderful it is to see your own sweet little kids, to feed them, and to teach them about life."

"What nonsense," replied the spider.

"That's nature's way," argued the mouse. "And despite what you say, I'll do what I can to help. On my route along the fence, every day I see plenty of spiders. You're right; they are much smaller than you but otherwise good-looking. Maybe I'll meet a big one. I'll mention to them that a lovely princess is sitting here longing for a suitor."

"Then you'll be telling a terrible lie," squealed the spider much amused, and then she looked serious again. "And don't bother searching for a male larger than me. All our males are pitiful, small weaklings. Nobody pays them any attention. In our species, only the females are worth anything."

"Well, I will look anyway," insisted the mouse, "I'll find you the right one. I can't believe you won't become the most lovable creature once you've fallen in love."

"Oh, run along, little mouse," said the spider with a wave of two of her legs. "No male alive can bring me any pleasure. But you don't see that because you have nothing else in your head but love and silly twaddle."

With that, she killed a fly, spun a case around it, hung it up, and then hid under a leaf. The mouse scurried away, and the wild parsley and wild carrot put their heads together and chattered about what they hoped the future would bring.

Chapter 5

The next morning, a handsome male spider was sitting on the wild parsley, but he was keeping his distance from the somewhat fierce-looking, large and not overly friendly female that was crouched on one of the wild carrot's leaves. He bent and stretched his legs out, so she could see that he had a rich endowment. Seven eyes were beaming with love while the eighth eye watched carefully that she didn't eat him.

"Permit me, madam, to offer you my hand and my heart," he said."He knows how to express himself," said the wild parsley.

"A wonderful male," gushed the wild carrot.

"I'm the one that lured him here," gushed the mouse, pleased with herself.

"The wimp," said the spider.

But the male spider didn't give in so easily. He pushed out his chest, now reserving two of his eyes to watch her carefully while his remaining six eyes beamed twice as much love as before.

"Don't think I have any intention of being a burden to you," he said. "I have my web on the fence a little distance from here and can catch the few flies I need. I now have five really fat fellows spun and hung, and it would be an honor for me to present them to you tomorrow so you can see... it is you alone that I love."

"Are you insane?" sneered Miss Spider. "What am I supposed to do with a jerk like you?"

"Good gracious," he said, and noticing how fiercely she glared at him, he now had only one eye filled with love for her. "But if my courting comes at the wrong time, I'll understand, and I will wait for another opportunity..."

"I suppose it's the safest thing for you," she said. "Make sure you clear out quickly, or I'll..."

In a flash, she launched herself at him, but he quickly lowered himself down on a thread and just got away, hiding in the undergrowth. A little later, she was sitting in her web looking angrier than ever.

"What a female!" said the mouse

"Yes, precisely," replied the spider.

"You don't have to take the first one that comes along," offered the wild parsley.

"He wasn't the right one," agreed the wild carrot.

By now, the unlucky suitor was running around the fence telling the other male spiders about this beautiful but strange female that had spun her web between the wild carrot and wild parsley.

"She is so big," he said, spreading his legs, four on each side, as far as he could. "I've never seen anyone so beautiful in all my days. But she's as proud as a peacock. I'll go to my death mourning over her refusal. I'll never have a mate now."

They all listened to him with bulging eyes and wanted to hear the story again. It wasn't long before the saga of the haughty and beautiful Spider Princess had swept down the fence row.

When the male spiders finished their day's work, they all gathered together and chatted about her. Every one of them had a comment to offer, but eventually, they all became so inflamed with love they thought it impossible to live unless they won the beautiful princess.

One after the other, they ventured out to court her, but it went miserably for all of them. The first of them was a handsome fellow who had mocked the previously unlucky suitor enormously because he had promised the spider princess the five thread-wrapped flies he had hanging home in his web.

"Young strong females don't give a hoot about those kinds of promises," he said. "They want a handout right away. Now look at me... at what I have," pointing a leg at a decidely large blowfly.

"Do I need a male to nourish me?" she mocked him, and before he could lose his look of surprise, she was upon him, and had eaten him instead.

Disrespectfully, she left the blowfly unattended until later in the afternoon when, thinking no one was watching, she gave in and ate it. And it went no better for the other suitors that came after the second one.

She ate six in the middle of their little speeches, and another two didn't even have time to open their mouths. A starling picked off one as he was taking his bow, and another one, after just looking at her, fell over from fright into the ditch where he drowned at once.

"That was twelve suitors," said the mouse as she looked down into the ditch and watched the unloved spider float away on the gentle current.

"I haven't been counting," replied the spider. "But maybe now I'll get some peace and quiet."

"You are a contemptible female," said the mouse. "I predict that you'll go childless to your grave."

For the first time, the spider looked a little concerned.

"It's too bad you can't have kids without having a male around," she mused.

"Oh listen! Her hard heart is melting," announced the mouse with a hint of sarcasm.

"Oh!" said the wild parsley, missing the point.

"Ah!" said the wild carrot.

"Oh, what silly talk!" said the spider, but she was thinking more about the matter and appeared increasingly worried. As she glanced at the combs in her claws, she hardly even noticed that a big, juicy fly had flown into her freshly repaired web.

"Let's face it," she muttered, perhaps more to herself than anyone else. "One should try to bring some capable offspring into this world—females I would hope. I suppose it's my duty to leave behind some heirs to express the contempt I have for those obnoxious males."

"She's on the way," whispered the mouse.

The wild parsley and wild carrot nodded, but neither of them said a thing so as not to interrupt her train of thought. However, the mouse scurried off to the fence and called all the surviving male spiders together.

"Whoever proposes to the princess tomorrow will get her," she said. "You won't recognize her. She's softened, and her heart is melting. She captures no flies, doesn't eat or drink; she sits and looks out longingly into space. Hurry up and get yourselves organized."

But the male spiders didn't seem so keen any more. They just looked at each other, their doubts showing on their troubled faces. There wasn't one of them that had courage enough to make an attempt at courtship, seeing as how badly it had gone for the other twelve. Several of the wisest among them descended immediately to the undergrowth to hide and avoid any temptation.

A few remained together to think over what the mouse had told them and to consider their options. Then finally, one lean young fellow, who had always only listened when the other males talked about the lovely princess suddenly spoke:

"I will try!" he announced proudly.

"You?" they all shouted together before they laughed at the suggestion that this little guy could achieve what so many brave and bigger males had given their lives for.

But he let them laugh as much as they wanted.

"I hardly think I'm meddling in any of your affairs," he said modestly. "None of you even want to dare, but I will attempt it.

I've looked her over, and she is a magnificent female. She's rejected twelve, so maybe she'll take the thirteenth. Besides, I don't think the others knew how to court her."

"Oh, is that right?" mocked one as the others continued to laugh. "What are you going to do?" asked another.

"Come along and see for yourselves," he said. "Tomorrow, I'm walking over and proposing."

Chapter 6

And so, he did. The following morning, he came strolling over on his eight legs, looking serious, but careful. Behind him at a little distance followed all the other male spiders that lived by the fence. The long twigs on the stumps stretched to see him, while the wild parsley and wild carrot broadened their leaves and flowers to allow him to move as easily as possible. Sheltered behind an old tree root, the mouse stood up on her hind legs, staring and listening intently.

The princess was sitting in her web, acting like she hadn't seen him.

"Noble Princess," the young spider said in a strong voice, "I'm asking you to accept me as your mate."

"Really?" she asked, pretending she wasn't interested, but she liked this one more than any of the others. They all wanted to make her their own—this one only asked to be her mate. That sounded more modest and pleasing.

"She will give in," said the mouse dancing with joy.

"Hush!" said the wild parsley.

"Quiet!" hissed the wild carrot.

"She hasn't eaten him yet," whispered one of the male spiders.

"I know you have had many offers," said the thirteenth suitor. "A simpleton like me is nothing compared to you, the largest and most amazing female on the whole fence. But that's why I'm attracted to you."

She turned around and gazed at him. He was ready to sink into the ground from fear and cast his eight eyes downward. All the other male spiders bolted away quickly.

"Now she's going to eat him," agreed the wild parsley and wild carrot.

"She's a sweet specimen," said the stump twigs.

"She's a horrible female," said the mouse.

But she didn't eat him. Instead, she grabbed a fly that had just flown into her web, bit it and sat back comfortably to consume it while observing him carefully. He looked more pitiful than ever, shaking as if his last hour had arrived. But she took a liking to him, thinking this was what a male should be. And when he saw that she meant him no harm, he relaxed and spoke to her again.

"I'm sure you don't consider me very attractive," he admitted. "I am what I am, just a simple fellow, but if I could be a father to a daughter who would look anything like you, I'd consider my life's goal accomplished and humbly give thanks for my good luck."

The suggestion of a daughter did it and the most wonderful thing happened. She grabbed a fly leg and threw it to him which, according to spider custom, is as good as saying, "yes."

Trembling from happiness and anxiety, he crept nearer to her.

"That's close enough," she said. "I've chosen you, but don't irritate me, or I will eat you."

"She chose him!" said the mouse who immediately fainted from joy.

"She chose him!" said the wild parsley and the wild carrot.

"She chose him!" said the twigs on the stumps, rustling with sheer amazement.

As soon as the successful suitor returned to his part of the fence, now feeling very proud of himself, he spread the word, and soon all the other male spiders knew what had happened. It surprised all of them, and they were jealous, but they organized a party to celebrate the news of his acceptance, and that she had not eaten the young spider. And what a party it would be.

The whole fence row was celebrating, but the mouse thought she was the happiest because it was all her doing. However, the wild parsley and wild carrot were equally happy because now they could expect what they had longed for the most, a growing family in their midst, allowing them to surpass their neighbors. Even the twigs on the old stumps were so happy they forgot to be jealous.

There wasn't any reason to have a long ceremony or engagement; that made little sense. The wild parsley and wild carrot scattered their white flowers everywhere to suggest a festive atmosphere, and the mouse brought her young ones up the fence to see the happy couple. The bluebell peeled, the poppy laughed, and the bindweed closed its petals for a while in order not to embarrass the new couple with its nosy curiosity.

The hungry spider ate all the flies she had wrapped up for later, offering none to her new mate, but the great happiness he felt so filled his throat he wouldn't have been able to swallow even a bite. He did as little as he could, but when she once stroked him on the back with one of her combs, he shivered in pure ecstasy.

Early the next morning, the mouse was there again, peering intently into the web.

"Have any of you seen the young couple?" she asked.

"No," replied the wild parsley.

"They're asleep," whispered the wild carrot.

"Oh," said the mouse, "what luck; we finally found her someone. Now you'll see how sweet and warm she can be. There are no limits to the wonders that love can achieve. And when the kids come ..."

"Do you think she'll sing, finally?" asked the wild carrot.

"I'm hoping for the best," said the mouse. "She doesn't seem to have a singing voice, but as I said—'love'! Now she will glow when she comes out. I hope we'll recognize her."

They all laughed together, and even the rising sun joined in. In fact, they made such a noise that the spider came crawling out of her leaf hideaway.

"Congratulations! Congratulations!" sang the mouse.

"Congratulations! Congratulations!" said the wild parsley and wild carrot.

The spider stretched herself and yawned and then sat in her web as though nothing had happened.

"Where is your mate?" asked the mouse. "Is he still sleeping?"

"I ate him for breakfast," replied the spider.

The mouse screamed so loud you could hear it down the whole fence row, and the wild parsley and wild carrot trembled so much that many of their flowers fell off. The twigs groaned as if a storm were raging.

"He looked so stupid and disgusting lying there next to me," said the spider. "So, I ate him. If he knew I was hungry, he would have stayed away from me."

"God help us!" screamed the mouse. "You ate your very own love!"

"Oh, no!" said the wild carrot and wild parsley together.

"Oh really, what nonsense," said the spider.

Chapter 7

For the following few days, all was quiet around the fence, and even the weather turned gloomy. The spider spoke to no one and attended to her web, catching and eating more flies than ever before. She looked so fierce that no one dared say anything to her. The male spiders stayed far away, but they gathered every evening to talk. The subject was how scary the Spider Princess was.

"Yes, but he won her!" said one of the most romantic.

But it incensed another, asking if being eaten by your mate the morning after the joyous celebration could be anyone's idea of happiness? He had no answer to that because his romantic feelings were not genuine. He was just glad he'd not been the one.

The mouse, head down, paced back and forth from her nest. She took it hard, as though something had happened to her own family. The wild carrot and wild parsley drooped their heads, feeling embarrassed and downcast in front of the twigs on the stumps. They were so depressed that even the twigs thought it was a shame to tease them about it.

One morning, when the sun was blazing down, the spider had crawled as far under her leaf for shade as she could. The wild parsley bent down to the mouse hole in the tree stump.

"Psst, little mouse," whispered wild parsley.

"What is it?" asked the mouse, poking her nose out of the hole.

"We want to ask you something because you're so smart—tell me—do you think the spider will act differently when it's time to lay her eggs?"

"I refuse to have any interest in anything more about her," said the mouse haughtily. "I don't think that female will ever lay any eggs."

But she did.

One beautiful morning, the spider acted in a way that no one at the fence would ever forget.

"Ugh!" she said, to anyone who might be listening. "To think I have to go through all this just to have offspring."

She marched up and down the leaves, spinning around in circles as if she couldn't get comfortable, and then she suddenly froze and out popped a clump of eggs, ten in total. The spider now spun around again and glared at them.

"Build a nest! Build a nest for them," twittered the wild parsley. "We have plenty of material for you."

"Sit on them and keep them warm," urged the wild carrot. "We'll weave a roof over you, so the sun won't bother you in the least."

"And you must capture flies for the kids when they hatch," said the mouse knowingly. "You do not understand how hungry kids can get."

"Practice singing to them a little," said the twigs on the stumps.

"What a load of nonsense," said the spider and turned her back on them as she laid four more clumps of eggs. When she had finished, she spun a fine cocoon of white thread around each clump.

"She's not completely without a heart," said the mouse.

The spider took the first cocoon of eggs, scurried down to the fence, and buried it in deep in the undergrowth. She went back up

to the web for another cocoon, and continued in this way until she buried all five cocoons.

"Well," she said. "That's it for me. Never again. Now I'm finally able to be a free and independent female again."

"A delightful female!" squeaked the mouse sarcastically. "Such a shameful creature and a disgrace to her gender."

"What a sweet little bird," interjected the twigs on the stump.

Neither the wild parsley nor wild carrot said anything the next morning about the missing spider. It upset them even to talk about it.

"The starling got her," said the mouse, sounding almost pleased. "One peck... gone. I saw it myself."

“We hope he doesn’t get a stomach-ache,” said the stump twig. “She had to be a bitter mouthful to swallow.”

Fall came and went, followed by winter. The mouse stayed cozily in her hole and the spider eggs lay snugly on the ground. The wild parsley and wild carrot withered and died, and the twigs on the stumps lost their leaves but rustled through the storms, the freezing weather, and the snows until the new spring arrived. Then the mouse first appeared again and wondered who might be around.

The Cuckoo's Dilemma

Chapter 1

Deep into the forest that stood at the edge of a lush green meadow, there was a large group of old hawthorn bushes in which the shrikes built their nests. They finished building them on the first day of May when the sun was shining brightly, and after sitting around and chatting for a while, mother shrike laid three beautiful eggs in her nest.

"Now remember this," she said to her mate, sighing. "I'm not a young flirt playig around anymore. It's tme to get serious."

Her mate tried his best to make her feel better, but she remained grumpy and refused to listen to him.

"You males are all talk," she muttered. "When are you going to take responsibility? Instead, you put us off with your yakking, and always leave it to us to sit on the eggs. Don't just sit there trying to look so affectionate—it doesn't impress me, and I'm getting fed up. Now hurry and catch me a nice fat fly."

But her mate never moved, and by the evening she'd really had enough.

"If I had only known, I'd never have chosen you as a mate regardless of how lovely you sang!" she yelled at him. "I can't stand this! I can't stand it anymore and I'm flying away!"

The male shrike listened patiently to her. He had experienced the same story with his other mates—shrikes take a new mate every spring—and knew she would soon get over it.

"Okay, why don't you take a little break? Go and visit someone," he suggested, trying to calm her down. "But please return home later and sit quietly or those eggs will never hatch. My previous mate..."

She cut him off. "Will you please stop telling me about your other mates!" she screamed, and then flew off without another word.

Worried that she might hurt herself because she was so angry, her mate took off after her.

Shortly after they left together, another bird arrived and sat at the edge of their nest peering in. It was a much bigger bird than the shrikes, gray-brown all over with light spots on her breast and abdomen. She was carrying an egg in her bill, which she laid down

carefully next to the others. It wasn't any larger than the other eggs and looked just like them.

For a brief moment, the strange bird lingered, looking sadly at the little cozy nest in which she had deposited her egg, then she spread her wings and flew further into the forest. Up in a high tree, her mate was waiting for her.

"Did you leave the egg?" he asked.

"Yes," she replied. "I put it with the shrikes' eggs in the hawthorn thicket. They are good-natured birds, and hopefully will be kind to our offspring."

"We can't do any more than that," he said. "Cuckoo! Cuckoo!"

And they both flew off.

When the shrikes returned home, they didn't notice there were now four eggs instead of three. First, neither of them was especially good at addition, and second, mother shrike was now feeling much better. She sat down gently on the eggs while her mate sang to her, his songs reverberating throughout the forest.

She looked after the nest diligently, keeping the eggs warm for fourteen days while, now better behaved, her mate flew here and there capturing flies, butterflies, and larvae for her. He pinned them up on thorns near the nest so she could easily pop over, snatch them up, and quickly return to the nest.

"You're actually a decent mate," she said, nodding to show her satisfaction. "But it's about time you fussed over me since they are your eggs, too."

In the morning of the fifteenth day, the eggs cracked open and there lay four naked hatchings with wide-open mouths, and yellow beaks. The shrike pair observed them carefully.

"They have no eyes or beaks yet," he said, "but they will come."

"How lovely they are," said mother shrike happily.

Her mate smiled, and said mischievously: "And you didn't want to sit on those eggs!"

"Nonsense!" she replied, insulted. "I never said that; I was just angry when you were so lazy. Now get these poor babies something to eat instead of sitting here making silly comments. They are opening their mouths so wide I can see right down into their precious little tummies."

So the shrike flew off, came back, and flew off again the whole day, and for many more days after that.

Every time he returned to the nest with some food, the youngsters screamed just as loudly, as if they could never get filled up.

But all four were not equally hungry. One of them was far greedier than the others, and it was also growing up to be much bigger and stronger.

“This one will be a clever shrike,” said father shrike, and stroked the youngster’s back with his beak.

“You mustn’t have favorites among your newborns,” replied mother shrike sternly. “But I think the smallest are the prettiest.”

One evening, father shrike was quite depressed, and talked to his mate who was sitting in the nest trying to keep the young birds warm.

“It’s very difficult having a big family,” he complained. “Usually, I like to look neat and tidy, but now there is never time to freshen up, and I think it’s been an eternity since I warbled a tune. It’s getting increasingly difficult to do anything but look for food for this hungry bunch. There is hardly a butterfly left, and this morning the chaffinches took a scrumptious larva right out from under my beak. You will need to give me a hand. A poor bird like me can't afford to let his mate stay home and make believe she's a princess."

"Do you think we raised spoiled offspring?" she asked. "And why are you so upset? All four of them have their down feathers now, so we can leave them alone in the daytime. Starting tomorrow, I can help you."

So, the following morning, both of the shrikes flew around the meadow and scurried about looking for food for the family. It did not matter how much they brought home, the youngsters screamed just as loudly, and poked at each other trying to be first to get the largest piece.

Chapter 2

One day, when the parents came home with their beaks full of food, there was a terrible commotion going on in the nest. With their stretched necks—something new for them—the little ones were all screaming at the same time. Because she was so hopeless at arithmetic, she didn't notice that something terrible had happened.

"Speak one at a time, so we can understand you," said mother shrike. "What's the problem?"

Finally, she learned that the largest youngster had shoved one of the smaller ones out of the nest. The little one had been lying in the grass squeaking so pitifully that a fox came around and ate it.

"He hit me first," moaned the biggest nestling. "I couldn't help it that he fell out of the nest."

"Well, I'll teach you," said father shrike, and he rushed at the big nestling.

But his mate pecked him in the neck and scolded him harshly.

"You should be ashamed of yourself for being so hot-tempered!" she shouted. "Are you going to abuse that innocent child? Don't you dare touch her! Don't you see she couldn't help what happened?"

And after they had cried over the dead one, they flew off to fetch more food. They soon forgot about the nestling they had lost because the remaining three had such enormous appetites; the parents were almost ready to call it quits. The biggest one continued to grow and was already twice as large as the remaining two who complained that she pushed them around in the nest and took their food.

"You all must try to be nice to each other until you can take care of yourselves," said mother shrike.

"If only they were nearly all grown up, we could go somewhere warmer," said father shrike, shivering.

A week passed, and then something happened that made the parents cry again. One day they came home to find that only the largest youngster was in the nest.

"Where are your siblings?" screamed mother shrike.

"I couldn't help it," peeped the youngster. "They fell out of the nest. I couldn't help it! I turned a little, and one of them fell over the edge, and I got so terrified, that I bumped into the other one and he fell out too. I couldn't help it. And then the fox came and ate them."

The poor parents sat and cried their hearts out.

"We built the nest too small," admitted father shrike finally. "But how was I to know I would have such a big youngster? It's plain creepy how quickly she grows."

"You should have disciplined her in time," said mother shrike, forgetting she had protected the big youngster the first time it happened. "Oh, my poor little precious darlings!"

"If only we can keep the last one," said father shrike. "Now be a good bird and remember that we have no one left but you."

The youngster promised she would be before immediately eating all the food the parents had brought.

"More food! More food!" she screamed. "I'm so hungry—feed me!"

And the shrikes bolted away to find more for her to eat.

It now seemed as if they brought more food to the nest than they had when all the youngsters were living, but she could never get enough. She grew and grew, and at last became so huge that she couldn't fit into the nest. So she crawled out of the nest and hunched down on a nearby branch.

"Good gracious, young one!" screamed mother shrike when she returned home and saw her sitting outside. "You'll fall down and break your neck."

"You're always scolding me," cried the unhappy youngster. "I couldn't stay in the nest. I'm always doing something wrong, but I can't help it. I wish I were dead. Do you have anything to eat?"

The two parents helped the youngster carefully down to the ground, told her to hide in the grass, and not to tweet so that the fox would not hear her. They brought her food over a hundred times every day, and still she continued to grow. Eventually, feathers grew on her throat and on her wings so she could flap them as she explored the meadow. The parents had to keep an eye on her and often had to call her whenever they had food.

It looked so strange when the three of them sat together, for now, the youngster was double the size of the shrikes. She was so large she had to lie on her belly so they could put food down into her mouth. Also, she had different coloring and was gray-brown all over with light spots on her breast.

Sometimes, the father shriek sat and observed the youngster for a long time.

"She resembles no one in the family," he said to his mate who was half asleep because she was so worn out. "We're not so large, and we don't have her colors either."

One morning the youngster snapped up a large, disgustingly hairy caterpillar crawling in the grass.

"Spit it out! Spit it out!" screamed mother shrike. "It's poisonous, and it can kill you!"

"Oh, I eat these all the time," answered the youngster calmly. "It doesn't affect me at all, and you don't give me enough to eat."

"A strange shrike," said father shrike, shaking his head.

She's no shrike at all," said a voice close by.

Father shrike looked up and spied an old wren sitting on a branch.

"Who isn't a shrike?" he asked.

"She isn't," repeated the tiny bird, pointing with her beak towards the large offspring.

"She's not a shrike at all? What do you mean? Didn't my mate lay the eggs herself in the nest and haven't we honestly and devotedly raised her? It's too bad her brother and sisters are all dead."

"Dead now, are they?" questioned the old wren. "Heavens! Well, sometimes that's how it goes. It's an old story and a nasty one."

"Tell me more," said the father shrike, and he flew up and sat next to the wren. His mate flew up with him while the youngster was sitting down in the grass listening.

"It's easily explained," said the wren. "But it would be better if others could listen along too. The younger generations gain a lot from listening to us old-timers."

The tiny wren cried out hard as she could and eventually a group of wrens, shrikes, larks, siskins, goldfinches, and many other small birds came flying in. They sat around in the bushes, looking at the old wren, and listened intently.

"Do you know a large gray bird that sometimes sniffs around your nests?" asked the old wren.

"I know it well; it's a hawk," said a young goldfinch who thought he knew everything.

"No, smarty-pants!" said the wren, "but I only wish you were right. It would have been better for us, for then the predator would have eaten us immediately—end of story. That predator uses us and our nestlings for its own benefit, like we take flies and larvae to ours. For them, it's only fair play, and it's the way nature works, and besides, there's nothing we can do about it, even if it's not so nice for those of us who don't make it."

"Well, who is it then?" asked the goldfinch indignantly.

"We call the bird I'm talking about a *cuckoo*. They look almost like a hawk, but aren't such a bold bird, let alone an honest one who fetches food for their young. They're real sneaks, lazy good-for-nothings who fly around in the forest showing off and calling 'Coo-Coo' or some other such nonsense and..."

"Oh, I've heard those," interrupted the goldfinch and the others looked a little annoyed.

"Yes, well... so have many others, but they might not know who is making the call. Anyway, the cuckoos never lay even two straws on top of each other, never mind building a nest like us decent birds. The female never sits on her eggs, never keeps her youngsters warm from the cold nights, and would never push a fly down into their small yellow throats."

"Good gracious!" said mother shrike. "What does she do?"

"Well, now," replied the old wren, "this is the story: As soon as she has laid an egg—on the ground will do—the cuckoo takes it in her beak and flies with it to the nest of a good-natured bird pair. Without realizing there is another egg in their nest, this pair nurtures the cuckoo's egg and feeds the youngster along with their own. They do not understand how much they will work themselves to the bone providing the beast with enough to eat. And do you know what thanks they get for their loving attention? You guessed it; the cuckoo youngster takes the food from the others, and when it has grown up enough, it shoves the other youngsters out of the nest to make itself more comfortable. There, now you have the story."

The small birds sat on the branches shaking. The shrike pair couldn't believe what they heard from the wren, and all their feathers were standing on edge from fright.

"Look at those two over there," said the wren, and pointed to the shrikes with her wing. "They have taken care of a cuckoo's youngster all summer. See how thin and worn out they look. Ask them where their own small, young ones have gone. But if you

want to see their rotten foster child, look down in the grass where she's stuffing her enormous beak with food."

All the birds looked down at the young cuckoo and let out a loud cry.

"Cuckoo-brat! Cuckoo-brat!"

The young cuckoo quickly swallowed another hairy caterpillar and ran further out onto the meadow, turned around, and screamed back:

"It isn't true, I am not an evil bird, and I am not ungrateful!"

But the other birds flew down after her, wanting to peck her to death. At the head of the flock, there was the young goldfinch who screamed much louder than all the others. At the rear were the two shrikes, still confused by what they had heard, but they pleaded with the other birds not to do anything to the cuckoo youngster.

"She's all we've got left!" shrieked mother shrike. "And I have hatched her out; we have fed her and brought her up. In a way, she's still our own little precious daughter."

The cuckoo youngster gave the goldfinch a push with her beak so it stumbled.

"I'm big enough to defend myself," she said. "I can see that you're all against me, so I'm going away. I thank my foster parents for what they did for me, but I don't believe the old wren's story. And I will find out the truth about all this if I have to travel to the end of the earth."

So she flew away, over the meadow and over the great forest. Even as she was flying, she noticed from the strength of her wings she was now all grown up. She flew over fields, over other forests and meadows where the farmers were stacking hay; she flew far away to foreign lands.

And every time she rested, she mulled over the story she had heard. She could not understand it; it was not believable. She knew she was not any worse than other bird, and could not grasp why her real mother let her grow up with everyone hating and despising her. She wondered if she might meet up with her real mother one day and get it sorted out.

Chapter 3

Back where she came from in Denmark, winter had arrived. The leaves had fallen from the trees, and the green meadow was hiding under a thick blanket of snow. In the forest, the hawthorn bushes stood up like sticks, and here and there on the twigs, there was a berry shriveled from the frost.

With no flies or larvae, there weren't many birds left from the summer, only the sparrows, chaffinches, great titmice, and the large black crows that squawked and flapped their wings to keep warm. The wren, the shrikes, the goldfinch, and all the other birds had flown down south where the sun is warmer, and the leaves are always green.

Also down in the warmer regions, the young cuckoo sat in a tall tree on Christmas Eve and gazed sadly out over the meadow. The sun was going down, and a thousand flowers were shining radiantly. But the cuckoo wasn't really seeing all this. She had not found her mother, nor had she forgotten the wren's story. But she had met three other cuckoos who had experienced the same upbringing, and she decided she was a member of a hated race that didn't even deserve to see the sun.

While she was sitting, depressed thinking about this, there was a rustling in the leaves next to her, and a large, old cuckoo stuck her head out and looked at her.

"You don't seem happy," said the old-timer. "Why are you so sad? Isn't it warm enough? Not enough food?"

"I'm looking for my mother," answered the young one.

The old cuckoo hopped along the branch next to the young one and studied her carefully.

"Perhaps I'm your mother," she suggested. "I saw you earlier in the grove and have been watching you here for a while. Something in my heart tells me you are one of mine."

"If you are my mother, you haven't got a heart at all," accused the young one. "My mother is a nasty bird, and she has hurt me."

"Really? Tell me more."

As she told her story, the old cuckoo listened carefully, and nodded occasionally to show she understood.

"In a hawthorn bush, you say," said the old one when the young cuckoo had finished. "In a large forest up in Denmark? Well, it all fits together, and you are my daughter. My how you've grown so big, so lovely!"

She stroked her lovingly on the wing with her beak, but with a loud cry, the young one flew off to another branch and shook her feathers.

"Don't touch me!" she shouted. "You're a nasty bird, and I hate you!"

"Dear me!" said the old cuckoo, not seeming to worry about her daughter's rage. "Let me tell you... now, I remember it as though it were yesterday, how I flew around with the egg—that was you inside—searching for a nest. I had to find one where the eggs already there resembled my own, for otherwise the returning birds would have discovered you and removed you from the nest. I took a long time, and I became so tired; I was afraid that I would lose the egg."

"I wish you had!" screamed the young one. "Then I would never have been born, would never have caused my brother and sisters to die, would not have caused so much pain to my poor, caring shrikes, would not have heard my mother scolded for being a rotten, lazy bird without having the chance to say one word in her defense!"

The old cuckoo said nothing, but just gazed sadly at her angry daughter.

"Why didn't you build a nest like other decent birds?" asked the young one. "And sit on the eggs and bring us food? Why? Why?"

The old cuckoo shook her gray head mournfully.

"All of us have to come to terms with our fate," she said sighing, "and I with mine. It's not so easy to be a cuckoo, believe me. But you'll come to understand this when you go back north to Denmark in the summer and lay your own eggs."

"Do you think I will behave so disgracefully?" demanded the young one disrespectfully.

"Do you really believe I wouldn't have rather built a nest and had my nestlings near me until they grew up and flew away out into the world?" asked the old cuckoo now a little indignant. "Do you think every summer I place my eggs in the nests of strange birds without a lot of regret? Never to know what has become of them?"

"Then why do you do it?" asked the daughter, now totally confused.

"Because there's no other way," advised the old cuckoo, "and no one knows about it but us, and it is very sad."

She flew over to the branch where the young cuckoo was sitting and settled next to her.

"Let me tell you how it is for us. We cuckoo mothers don't lay a clutch of eggs like most birds, but only lay one egg every eight days. So, this means that the first egg would rot before I laid the next one. That's because we'd have to fly away from the nest frequently to locate hairy caterpillars. We can't brood and hatch the babies out ourselves. Understand... it's impossible to find food for ourselves and the nestlings and also sit on the new eggs, hatching about 8 days apart... all at the same time.

"Then why don't you lay your eggs faster?" asked the young cuckoo. "Don't you care? The wren said you were just lazy."

"Oh, I do care!" insisted the old cuckoo. "I'd like so much to lay my eggs faster. There isn't anything I wouldn't do if only I could hold on to my own nestlings. But I can't. There is only enough room for one egg at a time in my body, and each egg takes eight days to form."

The young one still looked suspiciously at her.

"I don't believe you," she said firmly. "You're just making it up. The shrike isn't half as large as you, and she lays her eggs in a jiffy."

"Yes, she does," agreed the old cuckoo, "and she is lucky that she can. But she doesn't eat large, poisonous caterpillars like we cuckoos do either. There isn't much meat on them, and so we have to consume many, requiring our stomachs to be large, and therefore there is not much room left in our bodies for the eggs."

"Are you telling me the truth?" asked the young cuckoo.

"Yes," replied the old cuckoo. "That's just how it is. One fact follows from the other. If you understand it, then you can bear it, and it's never as mean-spirited as it seems."

"Well then, I can't blame you," said the daughter after thinking about it for a while. "And I'm sorry I have been so angry with you. But I also think it's a real shame that the other birds don't know; that is why they don't understand."

The old cuckoo stared ahead and then said: "It's like that often in this world. Everybody talks according to their understanding of things, and there is nothing else to do but let them talk. You can accept this if you have a clean conscience, and you do your work. And the duty of the cuckoo in nature is to eat hairy caterpillars."

As the sun went down and darkness arrived, the two cuckoos stayed in the tree discussing their lives and caterpillars for a long time. When they finally went to sleep, the young daughter dreamed about flying around the forest with an egg in her beak looking for a goldfinch's nest to put it in. The old cuckoo dreamed that the time had come when she wouldn't have any more youngsters to worry about, or to even feel sorry for their future.

Why The Mighty Oak Fell

Chapter 1

Every tree in the forest, every stem of grain, and every worm—all are equally worthy and have an undeniable right to life. But not all of them are equally lucky. Some of them keep cover, unnoticed in their hiding places, and afraid someone may see them. Others tower so high in the air you can see them from far away. Some are so shy they don't want you to know they even exist. Others are so proud, knowing how important they are, and are critical of everybody else.

The proudest creature in the forest is the oak tree and rightly so, with its ancient origins going way back before any of the other trees existed. It ruled the forest thousands of years ago when there were animals and trees which are now either extinct or have permanently migrated to foreign lands.

The oak can tell us a lot of strange stories, passed down the generations. There's the one about the bear that terrified the little fox, or another one about the elk that made the roe deer feel all tiny and insignificant. And there are more, but then the oak tree is enormously old.

As they grew up, the other trees could not believe what the oak told them about its experiences, and how the forest appeared in the good old days when there weren't any forest rangers, and everything grew here, there and everywhere. But the oak told those tales only in the wintertime when it had nothing to do, and when freezing weather penetrated deeply into the roots, and storms slammed into its branches. You need a good story at those times to cheer yourself up.

But the oak is a lot stronger than the other trees, and it can bend and gnarl its branches as much as it wants. Regardless of what you might think, the oak tree remains the noblest tree in the forest, and it knows this, proud of its reputation. It knows its position in the forest, but it also cares about others and is never critical of them. You would never see the oak acting so disgracefully that it would not let another tree get started. It welcomes everyone even though there are many who abuse its generosity. But it stands its ground powerfully, never forgetting who it is.

One day, a cuckoo sat on the top of the oak tree. It had happily laid its last egg in the shrike's nest and was free to do what it liked. The hairy moth larvae, its favorite food, was forming pupae, so the cuckoo was considering whether it was time to head south. But before it decided, it gave the oak tree a good piece of advice.

"Listen to this, my good oak tree," the cuckoo said. "Have you noticed how many beech trees are shooting up around you?"

"How could I miss seeing them?" replied the oak. "They're already tall enough that they have shaded my lower branches and are already hurting them. And lots of my acorns are not sprouting, because those beeches shade them from the sun."

"Well, aren't you going to do something about it?" questioned the cuckoo. "As big and noble as you are, you must know they are a danger to you. They will grow faster than you can imagine, and they will happily choke you. I am always looking around in this world, as you know, and I've seen a lot of oak trees succumb to those pesky beeches."

"Oh, nothing will choke me," answered the oak confidently. "My roots reach deeper into the soil than theirs, and my crown reaches higher in the sky. Besides, what should I do?"

"You need to attack them with their own weapons; cast shadows over them, grow faster and smother them," suggested the cuckoo.

"That's something I'd never do," replied the oak, a little taken aback. "You want me to overlap my leaves close together—me? Are you suggesting I should rush around like I'm a criminal, and end up with sick and weakened twigs? No, no, my good cuckoo. I don't accept all this modern craziness. I'll position my leaves so they don't get in the way of each other. I'll patiently twist my branches slowly and deliberately, which I learned from my forefathers, who told me how to behave like a respectable oak as I get bigger."

"You're just an old-fashioned relic," said the cuckoo and it flew off to Italy.

"Might I suggest you should consider what the cuckoo told you?" inquired a nightingale that was sitting in a thicket of beech trees and had overheard their conversation.

"There's nothing to think about," insisted the old oak. "I don't like that sort of behavior. I am who I am, and I'll never change. I am the noblest tree in the forest, and I must uphold my position."

"But you're all washed up, oak tree!" mocked the young beeches together. "Your time has come and gone. You don't have a chance, anymore. Just wither away quietly or we'll arrange it for you."

The oak did not respond because a noble tree does not argue with its inferiors. As for so many years before, it stood its ground quietly but with strength until its acorns were ripe and it let them fall to the ground.

"Godspeed, my seeds," it said, "and be shining examples of an oak tree... or perish."

"Die! Die!" screamed the beeches. "We'll choke every last one of them as soon as they peek up from the ground."

Chapter 2

Fall arrived, and the leaves of the beeches and the oak and most of the other trees fell, all except the spruce that whistled and sang. But nobody envied it because it did not have the best of summers since the other trees were both greener and prettier; now, it was feeling cheerful again. The flowers were withering in the meadow, and the birds that couldn't find anymore to eat, and had enough strength and courage, left to find a warmer home for a while.

The mice remained in their winter hiding place, pleased with all that they had stowed away. The ants escaped from the outside world in their anthill; the badger was already in hibernation; the fox was starving. And all the while, the old oak continued telling stories from the past like it always did, and everyone listened, even the spoiled, naughty young beeches.

Then it was soon early in March, and spring was coming even if it was not yet so obvious. There were still piles of snow, and it was freezing cold. Whatever the buds were thinking, they kept it to themselves. The smartest ones were swelling, but no one thought it was time to bud out. When the sun shone nice and warm in the afternoon, the anemones down under the ground felt a little urge in them. But they settled down comfortably because they also knew if they sprung up too early, they wouldn't make it.

While the oak had no concern about the spring, the beeches were mocking it.

"You're waking up too late, old oak," said the beeches. "You're always too late. Watch out that springtime doesn't pass you right by before you know it. Or maybe you don't even care to bud out this year? Maybe you're dead already?" The oak said nothing, but meanwhile, a strange little critter was sitting on one of its branches.

With delicate, transparent wings, and a waist like a hornet, everyone that knew about forests figured out immediately that it was a wasp. But no one could figure out what in the world it was doing at this time of the year, and the chaffinch, which really was longing for some insects to eat, was so astonished to see it; it completely forgot to snap it up.

"May I?" asked the wasp.

"How can I help you?" replied the old oak.

"If it's okay, I'd like to deposit my egg in one of your buds?" asked the wasp.

"If it's only that, then please be my guest," answered the oak. "But isn't it kind of early for you to be flying around? And who are you by the way?"

"Oh, I'm the galling wasp," the insect replied. "I have to begin my work early. Otherwise, the galls won't be ready in time."

"Why do you want to lay your egg in that old fellow?" yelled the nearest beech. "He will not bud out before mid-summer if he buds out at all. Come on over to us, instead. We're young and vibrant, and by early May, we're all leafed out if everything goes well."

"Thanks, but I'm fine where I am," replied the gall wasp.

"Do as you please," said the oak. "I'm the oldest and most distinguished tree in the forest, and I can house you easily. Also, I don't pry into others' business."

Meanwhile, the gall wasp was penetrating its stinger into the bud and bore into it. That went slowly because the bud scales were hard as seashells.

"Our buds are softer!" shouted the beeches and shook their branches, but no one answered them. "Who in the world knows what kind of creature that gall wasp is? It's very suspicious that it sneaks around during winter. Besides, its larva will probably destroy the leaves... it will serve that old oak right, the show-off."

Just then, a dewdrop fell from the oak's crown right onto the bud where the gall wasp was sitting, and it remained hanging. The gall wasp went into it with its wings and legs, said nothing, but kept right on boring in. When the moon came out early in the evening, the droplet had transformed into a little piece of ice, and the gall wasp was sitting inside the ice.

"Bad luck," said the old oak.

"Didn't we say it would end badly," scoffed the beeches.

"I should have eaten it," sighed the chaffinch.

That night, everyone in the forest talked about the terrible tragedy that had befallen the poor wasp and the oak tree could not remember telling a stranger tale.

The next morning, the sun was warming everything up, and the ice melted rapidly.

"Let's start again," said the gall wasp, adjusting its wings and legs.

"Will wonders ever cease?" gasped the oak, thinking it really had a good new story to tell.

Everyone thought likewise. But the gall wasp did not care about their astonishment or questions; instead, it kept on boring into the bud until the hole was large enough for it to lay its egg. Then it flew away and died somewhere in the sunshine.

Chapter 3

When spring arrived, the oak was the last tree to break out in bud. It waited until the weather was pleasant and reliable before bursting out with its lobed leaves. They appeared slowly in a controlled way, yellow in the beginning, then gradually enlarging and becoming green.

"I will build my nest high on your crown," said the father eagle. "I'm king of the birds as you are king of the trees."

"Okay, that's fine. Build it where you want," replied the old oak. "My house is open to everyone."

The eagle and his mate built its nest, and the young ones came out of the eggs, making an awful commotion. Their poop messed up the oak's branches, causing many to wither and die. When the eagle parents returned after finding food, they broke branches flapping with their broad wings as they hopped from branch to branch until finally settling down for the night.

"That's a lovely family the oak tree has," the beeches said laughing.

But the oak was polite and hospitable to everybody; there wasn't any other tree in the forest that could accommodate the mighty eagles.

As summer progressed, more and more creatures came around asking for space, and they all got it. The oak flea came, a little nimble beetle which laid its eggs on the midrib of the leaves. A couple of days later, the young ones were born and ate continuously until they had consumed the entire leaf.

Then a little moth showed up, and did the same thing. A lot of other critters arrived and sometimes the oak's leaves were so infested it almost could not catch its breath. But it said nothing, only nodding to its own family, the young oaks growing nearby. The old oak just told them it was the obligations of the nobility.

But the leaf that the gall wasp had penetrated while it was still a bud had five large galls on it, that looked like berries. Inside each gall, there was a little white grub, and the galls were so bitter that not even one bird wanted to eat them. And so nothing disturbed the larvae until the leaves fell off in the fall, and the adult gall wasps broke out of the galls.

"Thanks for the comfortable lodging," they said to the oak.

"You're welcome," replied the oak. "Maybe it's time now to settle down with a mate?"

"We don't work that way," said the new-generation adult gall wasp.

"Good heavens," said the oak, looking lovingly at its own young family growing underneath it. "It must be sad to go through life without kids."

"Oh, we have kids," said the gall wasp. "We can do a lot more than that."

"What did you say?" asked the oak surprised. "Can you have kids without mating? I recall that your mother froze inside some ice and didn't even get a cold from it. You're a strange family."

"In March, we'll be back and lay our eggs in you," said the young wasps.

"You are welcome, always welcome," replied the oak.

As it was now well into the fall, nearly all the leaves had dropped, but there remained a solitary one, fluttering about at the end of one of the oak's larger branches. In the middle, there was a queer little yellow spot, almost covered by what looked like a tiny felt blanket. The oak wondered what it was; it had never seen that before. Then a weak sound came from underneath the blanket.

"Do you have any buds for me, dear old oak?"

"Buds?" said the oak. "My leaves have just fallen, so it's too early to be thinking of buds. I have them for next year, but they are so unbelievably small now."

"They're big enough for my siblings and me," said the weak voice. "You have absolutely no idea how small we are."

"I can't even see you," said the oak.

"No one can see us," said the voice. "Not without a magnifying glass. We are the gall mites. We've been hiding the whole summer under the felt on this leaf, having a great time. But now we're getting

cold, and so we thought it would be all right to go into your buds to spend the winter. You've got buds' scales around them, right?"

"I have," said the oak. "But that's not what they're for. The gall wasps put their eggs there, so isn't that generous enough of me? Can't you crawl down into the ground or pupate in my bark or some other place?"

"We never pupate," explained the mite. "We are all identical and only become larger gradually as we eat. We have an unusually big mouth to drag around on spindly legs, so we can't run around everywhere. And we have no wings, so we can only sneak under a bud scale and spend the winter there. Next summer, we'll come out again into the open and lie under the felt blanket on one of your leaves."

"Whatever it takes," answered the oak. "I have never refused help to anyone. Be my guest."

The little ones crawled into the buds, where they could hide. But while the storms of the fall raced through the forest, the oak finally decided it had to think about its future, and it did not like what it was seeing.

That year the oak had only produced half as many acorns as was usual. It had a hard time sucking up all the nutrients through its roots and three of the large branches lowest down had died because the beeches had shaded them. But what was the worst of all, it had an eerie feeling in the middle of its trunk.

"Am I about to become hollow?" said the oak to itself, and the answer was... yes.

There was a somewhat large place where the bark had peeled off, and the tree had rotted. One day, when the buck deer was rubbing the downy layer on its new antlers against the bark, large chips had fallen out from the oak's trunk.

"You're getting old," the buck had said.

"Well, I'm hundreds of years older than you are," replied the proud oak.

"Old Timer! Old Timer!" screached the beeches together, and the willows and the elder bush, the ash, the rowan tree and even the alder bushes, so weak they constantly had to stand with their roots in the water, all joined in with tormenting the old oak.

Now, as the fall brought its usual changes, a little long-tailed field mouse came scurrying by.

"Do you mind if I build myself a nest inside you?" it asked.

"Well, I don't think I have anything vacant, but be my guest if you can find somewhere," replied the oak. "Winter is coming, and I would never refuse a fellow creature a place to live."

"I'll build my own place," said the mouse.

The mouse dug into a rotting part, letting the chips of wood fly left and right. After just a few minutes, the only part of the mouse you could see was the end of its tail.

"Pardon me," said the oak politely, "but isn't the hole large enough for you yet? It hurts a little when you gnaw into my good parts."

"I'll need space for my dining room," said the mouse.

"Yes, you do I suppose," replied the old oak.

And the mouse set up a very nice and spacious store, filling it with beechnuts, hazelnuts, and acorns.

"Would you mind not eating my acorns?" said the oak. "You are living here rent-free!"

"Oh, I need to gather what I can," argued the mouse. "There are so many mice in the forest, and they're all hungry."

"Of course," sighed the oak quietly.

Chapter 4

Over the following winter, the old oak sighed often, creaking inside. The wind had torn off a large branch, and its stories about the good old days weren't fun anymore. When spring arrived again, the gall wasps returned, along with more noisy beech and the eagle, the mites and the oak fleas, and all the other creatures. And the old oak was not feeling well.

It didn't have so many leaves as usual, and most of them were small and never turned green. The only ones that looked about right were at the top of the tree. The beech trees stretched their branches so far down that even fewer of the younger oaks' branches got any sunshine so their buds could not break out. And what was the worst? That hole the mouse gnawed out for itself was now full of water.

In early spring it rained a lot, and every time the water dried up, new rain came. The old oak could feel it was rotting away as the hole got larger and larger. And that... it knew for sure... was a sign it was sick and dying. But no one living in it ever bothered to notice.

Never had there been so many gall wasps as this year and nearly every single oak leaf was full of red and yellow galls. At the very highest twigs, the galls were so thick that the twigs bent down from the weight. There weren't even many leaves where the gall mites did not spread their felt blankets, and up in the eagle's nest, there was one more nestling than the past year, and they were causing a terrible racket.

"Don't take offense," said the old oak, wanting to talk to as many of its lodgers as possible, "but I'm not as strong as I used to be. I'll do what I can to be the good host, but if you could all not gnaw on me as much and treat my twigs more gently. Please?"

"Just listen to that old timer!" shouted the beeches triumphantly. "Finally, he's giving up. How important is he now, and what's become of his nobility?"

"I'm not giving up," replied the oak proudly. "I'm as good as I've always been, and I won't yield an inch to you. My family has ruled the countryside before you were born, and I was a mighty tree while you were barely a seed," said the oak before he added more quietly, "but I can't compete with you, I admit."

"No, you can't," said the uncaring beeches, laughing, "because we're smarter than you."

"Perhaps," said the oak. "You can describe it any way you want, but I don't know of any other trees under my shadow. I belong to the old school, but I can't fight against these new circumstances. My acorns don't have those stickers that can attach themselves to the fur of the fox wanting to rest under my crown. I don't awaken my buds purposely so they are the first ones to sprout in the spring, but instead, I take my time so they can settle in and become strong. That's the way I'm made; it's in my upbringing and in my memories, and it's all about the obligations of the nobility."

"Ha, ha, ha!" giggled the beeches.

But now the young oak tree growing nearby groaned and moaned something awful.

"Oh, I'm dying," gasped the young oak. "I'm really struggling to live. I get too little sunshine, and the gall wasps weigh down my branches to the ground. I can hardly breathe. What am I going to do? Oh, what can I do?"

"If it's time to die, then you will die," admitted the old oak sadly. "Perhaps this old, distinguished family's time is up, and now those who don't care will take over. I don't know. Deep inside, I feel like I am dying, but, I expected my descendants would survive me and keep the family line going."

"You are dying because you can't cope," said the beeches gleefully. "Now it's our turn."

"Just ask the humans if I can cope," argued the oak. "Ask them where they get their lumber from, wood that lasts. With your miserable wood, they can only get firewood and cheap furniture that common folks use. But from me, they create beautiful furniture and planking for ship decks and costly things that get handed down from family to family."

But the beeches just laughed at the oak, and finally, they stopped talking altogether. Everyone that lived in the oak tree was doing well, and they didn't care to think about the possibility that life was going downhill for their host. But in the quiet of the evening, the young oak complained to the old one.

"What a shame I have to die," said the oak sapling. "I am so young, and I had dreamed about becoming the fantastic tree you are, the greatest in the whole forest. You mentioned yourself the thousand-year-old oaks that folks from far away came to see."

"And I didn't lie to you," answered the old oak. "But I'm not the ruler of the world. Everything moves so fast these days, and that's not something planned in our make-up. Did you hear what the gall wasp said? They have their offspring without mating. How can we compete against that? We provide our pollen and eggs, and the wind flies around carrying the pollen, so the eggs get fertilized, making seeds. That's how it has always been for us, and we can't lower ourselves. Thank goodness, there are still other honorable trees around us in the forest that think like us. What would happen if we set a bad example, we oaks who are the noblest of them all? It's better that we die."

"Yes, I suppose so," admitted the young oak. "But it's very sad."

"Obligations of the nobility," pronounced the old oak proudly, determined to do its best, but it was all very difficult.

Chapter 5

Every year, the hole in the old oak's trunk grew larger. The rainwater filled it up until the trunk of the tree rotted, right down to the taproot. Woodpeckers were pecking away, and then came the bark beetles, the deathwatch beetle, and the longicorn beetle, and all of them laid eggs in the rotting wood. The young ones gnawed passages, here, there, and everywhere, under the bark and right into the heartwood.

"We must say, old oak, you're so delightfully soft… it's a real feast to munch on you."

"Sure, I am soft," said the oak, "but not so soft that I wouldn't offer hospitality to my friends. I can't refuse you anything I gave to others. As long as there is a scrap of life left in me, I'm open to any self-respecting fellow creature."

Meanwhile, the hole had spread so far that you could walk right into it. Soil got into it, too, and grasses and brightly colored flowers were growing, among them a sweet, white anemone that turned its heads towards the sun.

"Dear old oak, does it bother you I'm taking up space here?" inquired the anemone. "I can be in flower so much longer here than under the beeches where my sisters are. The beeches shade the sun from me as soon as they bud out into leaf, but you aren't nearly as mean."

"Oh, I'm not like that," said the oak. "It's an honor to be a safe place for such a lovely little flower. And I get real joy from saving someone from those nasty beeches."

A little rowan tree was growing up alongside the trunk, along with an ivy plant that was wiggling its way up to the top of the oak.

"You're just making me green again," said the oak cheerfully. "I won't produce any more flowers myself, but yours are greenish-yellow like mine, which lets me dream about the days when I was young."

"You're fine just as you are," said the ivy. "Great to put my arms around, great for a vine like me to support myself."

The beeches had now extended their branches so far down over the oak tree that there was always shade at the bottom. All the young oaks had been smothered, some withering sticks for trunks, while others had just perished and disappeared from the earth.

In the fall, only a few acorns from the oak tree fell to the ground through the thicket of beech branches, and none of them ever sprouted. Then, early one November morning, an owl appeared and checked out the hollow oak tree.

"It's nice here," the owl said. "Wonderfully dark inside and shady outside. I can't stand the daylight."

"I'm happy that I have a space you like," said the oak, "even if it is costing me my life. But keep using me as long as I'm here."

More owls came until they formed a colony. Bats also arrived, and they hung all day long on their hind legs with their heads pointed down, wings folded, and flew away when it got dark in the forest.

"I suppose I've become a safe place for a bunch of thieves," said the old oak, "but that's fine, one creature is as good as another. I won't judge anyone. Let each one look out for itself."

"You are in ruins," mocked out the beeches. "All kinds of low-life hide themselves in you now."

"If only you beeches would leave me alone," said the old oak sadly.

* * *

Finally, one summer arrived when the old oak could not send out any buds at all. Its crooked, grooved and gray old branches without a single leaf were sticking up through the light young beech foliage. All around, the flowers were fragrant, the birds were singing, and everything alive was green and happy. Except for the old oak tree.

"The oak tree is dead," said the beeches. But that wasn't quite true.

At the highest point on the oak tree, one tiny twig, like a young sapling, still had some fresh leaves. There weren't many of them, but together they created a sense of new green life, and the oak displayed them with dignity and pride.

"It's my banner," said the oak, "representing my old noble family. It will wave from my crown to my last day and announce to the whole forest that the old oak tree held out in good times and bad."

Both wasp galls and the mites' felt blankets filled those few leaves left at the top of the oak, which was enormously pleased that its guests were staying with it to the end.

"As long as I have a morsel of food, I'll share it with you," the oak said. "And I won't strangle anyone—unlike others around here—or encroach on anyone's boundaries, or mind others' business. When

I'm gone, you'll all miss me and say I was a good neighbor these eight hundred years I stood my ground in the forest."

And the oak seemed even happier when a large green woodpecker came by and began to build its nest in the trunk. The colorful bird, with his black patch over his eyes, merrily bored a hole where a dead branch had broken off and then his mate laid her eggs.

"Look at that!" said the oak happily. "I'm still good for something."

"You're still wonderful," said the father woodpecker. "There aren't any larvae left in you because your wood is too dry, so you're not a great place for eating. But in the old days, I dined superbly with you, and I'll never forget that. And so I will stay with you until you fall down."

"Thank you," said the oak.

That evening, some thirty crows came from the edges of the forest and sat on the oak's bare branches.

"If you don't mind," said the oldest crow sitting at the top of the oak, "we'll come here every evening and hold our meeting."

"It's a great honor," said the oak. "What is your meeting all about?"

"It's only local news and gossip," said the old crow, "but it always cheers us up after a hard day's work."

The next evening, a hundred crows arrived, and they made a terrible commotion, screaming, and fighting, and hopping around. It was much worse than when the eagles lived there, but the oak was happy despite the noise and the mess.

"They chose me above all the other trees in the forest," said the oak proudly.

"They chose you because your branches are bare," said the beeches. "You're dead, finished, and you can't hear what they are saying and can't see what they are up to. Whatever life you still have, they will take in a jiffy."

"I don't know why everyone chooses me," said the oak quietly. "But they do and you can't understand it because your only interest is in getting ahead by any means possible. I know I will die soon, but not for anything would I change places with you."

"Don't you have a bud for us, dear old oak," inquired the mites softly. "Soon, it will be fall, and we're getting cold."

"A bud... A bud?" said the oak, confused. "Yes, I have a bud, now let me see if I can find it ..."

The oak peeked at the leaf axils on the only green twig remaining. But there weren't any buds.

"I must have forgotten to get some started," the oak said with sadness. "I hope that's not a big inconvenience? I'm afraid I don't really know if I have anything left to make some for you. My roots are not functioning well enough to suck up anything, and my leaves have been so small this year…"

"Well, we have to die then," said the mites, which they did.

"This is disgraceful," said the oak, feeling both helpless and hopeless. "Imagine that I could forget to set buds! I even knew the mites were there, and now I'll never forgive myself that any guest of mine needed to die of hunger. Oh dear, age is catching up, and the end must be near."

"It is the end," scoffed the beeches. "You're going fast. When a tree doesn't set buds at the right time, then it means it's finished."

The oak didn't answer; it was so depressed. It shook its branches, and the last leaves dropped… they couldn't hang on.

Chapter 6

That winter there were terrible storms. Many proud trees fell, and more than one of the now dominant beeches struggled through. With the onslaught of wind and lightning, the old oak split and cracked from top to bottom. With a mighty roar, an entire half of the tree crashed to the ground, crushing an entire beech thicket as it fell.

And as the other half of the oak tree stood there, naked and empty, you could finally see how many creatures had lived inside it. Everywhere, there were grooves and holes where larvae and worms once were; it was a wonder that the old tree had not fallen a long time ago.

When springtime came, the surviving beeches had sprung out in bud, but the old oak tree was bare and gray. And now the beeches changed their tune.

"Break out! Break out!" insisted the beeches. "Let's see even one little leaf, you old fellow. Remember your noble obligations! A proud oak buds out in the spring!"

But the oak didn't respond... it was dead.

"There goes my house," said the owl.

"I no longer have my night lodge; it went with the oak," said the bat.

"There goes my nest," said the green woodpecker.

"I'll never have visitors again in my vines," said the ivy that had fallen down with the oak. Now torn into pieces, it was lying scattered around in a terrible mess. "Such a lovely old oak."

And the gall wasp, the oak fleas, the mites and mouse, the crows, the anemones and the still standing rowan tree, they all said the same thing. High in the sky, the eagle was hovering in flight and looking down on the dead oak.

"He was a noble creature," said the eagle, "right to the end."

Bang! Bang! The forester fired both barrels of his shotgun, but the eagle soared away, unharmed.

"Not yet Forester," said the eagle. "I've got to stay around a while, or the forest will become nothing but a bunch of creepy-crawlies."

The Combatting Queens

Chapter 1

The farmer opened his bee hive and looked down at a quiet scene. "Come on, you lot! Get out!" he told them. "The sun is shining, and the flowers are springing out everywhere; you'll have a lot of fun. Let me see how hard you can work by collecting lots of honey for me to sell, come the fall. Farming is in sad shape, and you all need to play your part. It takes many a small stream to make a mighty river."

"What do we care about your problems in farming," muttered the bees, but they flew out anyway.

After many hundreds of bees had fled the hive, at last the queen appeared. She was larger than all the others, and it was she who ruled over the hive. She flew around for a while and saw that all the bees seemed disorganized and not sure what to do. Having spent the whole winter cooped up in the hive, they were badly in need of a breath of fresh air. Humming and buzzing, they stretched their legs as they tried their wings and walked around on the ground before they flew off haphazardly to the flowers and bushes.

"Stop all this pointless buzzing here and there," she said, "and do something worthwhile. A good bee isn't lazy but seizes the moment and uses its time well."

She called them back to the hive and then organized them into groups.

"Now then, fly out and see if there is any nectar in all those colorful flowers," she said to the first group. "And you lot over there, collect the pollen, and when you get home, be sure to deliver it politely to the old bees inside the hive."

Those two groups flew off, but this still left all the youngest bees behind because they had never done any work before.

"What are we going to do?" they asked.

"You? You will sweat," said the queen. "One, two, three, all together now."

And they sweated as best they had learned, and a most wonderful yellow wax oozed from their bodies.

"Good job!" said the queen. "Now let's build!"

The older, resident bees took the wax and built a framework of small, six-sided compartments, each one identical and right next to the other. While they were busy constructing all this, the foraging bees came flying in with pollen and nectar which they laid at the feet of the queen.

"Let's knead the dough!" she said, "but first we need to put in honey to make it taste better."

So, on command, the older bees kneaded and kneaded and prepared lovely small loaves of bee bread which they carried into the beehive compartments.

"Now, let's build more!" ordered the queen bee, and so the youngsters sweated wax again, and built more compartments with a vengeance.

"I'd better start on my work!" said the queen sighing, because it was the hardest thing of all to do. She positioned herself in the hive's middle section and laid her eggs in large piles. The bees took the small eggs in their mouthparts and carried them into the new

compartments. Every egg had its own little room, and when they were all in place, upon the queen's command, the bees covered each room with a tight wax door to keep the eggs safe

"Well done!" she said when they had finished. "Now you can build me ten larger, more attractive rooms at the edge of the hive."

Because they were getting more proficient, the bees did this quickly, and in each of the large rooms, the queen laid a special egg before the bees attached a door.

"Keep safe and grow well my children," said the queen before she went to rest.

Chapter 2

With the youngsters now joining in, every day the bees flew in and out as they collected large amounts of nectar and pollen. Each night, with their work completed, they looked at all the eggs when the queen came by. One night, she told the bees the eggs' opening-up time had come.

"Watch out!" said the queen. "They're here!"

And all at once the eggs cracked open, and in every room, there lay a lovely newborn bee.

"What a bunch of funny creatures," said the young bees. "They have no eyes, and where are their legs and wings?"

"They are larvae," said the queen, "and you little greenhorns looked like that too, once. You need to be a larva before you can be a real bee. Now hurry up and give them something to eat."

The bees got busy feeding the little ones, but they did not pay equal attention to all of them. Those ten larvae in the big rooms got as much food as they wanted, and every day the worker bees gave them a larger portion of the nectar, now in the form of honey.

"They are princesses," said the queen, "so treat them especially well. With the others, you can limit their portions because they are just servants and have to get used to whatever comes their way."

And so, regardless of how hungry they were, the poor little larvae got just a tiny piece of bee bread every morning, and nothing more.

In one of the small, hexagonal compartments near the princesses' rooms, lay a very tiny larva. She was the youngest one of all and had only just recently broken out of the egg. She couldn't see yet but could hear what the older bees were saying while she lay there quietly, lost in her own thoughts most of the time.

"I would like to have more to eat," she said, and knocked on her door with her body.

"You've had enough to eat for today," answered one of the old bees, one designated the Maid of Honor, who was crawling up and down the passageways.

"But I'm starving!" cried the little larva, "and I'd like to have a room like the princesses; it's so cramped in here."

"Well, just listen to her," said the old bee sneeringly. "You would think she was a little fine princess the way she tells us what to do. You were born to work and toil, my little friend. You're just a simple worker bee, and you'll be nothing else your whole life through."

"But I want to be a queen," said the larva as she thumped her body against the door.

The old bee wouldn't dream of replying to such nonsense, and continued on to the others. Everywhere they were all screaming for more to eat, and the little larva could hear the whole thing.

"It's tough," she thought "to always be so hungry."

And so, she banged on the walls of the nearest princess, and yelled to her: "Give me some of your honey! Let me come visit you in your room! I am lying here starving, and I'm just as good as you are."

"Well, you wait until I am the reigning queen!" said the neighboring princess. "Believe me, I'll remember your insolence."

But hardly had she said this when the other princesses made an enormous fuss.

"You will not be a queen, I will, I will!" they all yelled, banging on their walls making a terrible scene.

The Maid of Honor came running over quickly and opened the doors.

"What has happened to Your Highnesses?" she asked, curtsying and fawning with her feet.

"More honey!" they all cried out together. "But, me first, me first; I will be the queen."

"At once, at once, Your Graces!" replied the Maid of Honor.

She scurried away as fast as her six old legs could carry her, and returned with many other bees who dragged a lot of honey with them. They stuffed this down the throats of the small, peevish princesses and gradually got them to calm down.

But the little larva was awake and was thinking over what had happened. She was longing for more honey and banged on her door.

"Give me more honey! I can't stand it any longer; I'm just as good as the others."

The old bee told her to be quiet.

"Be quiet, you little crybaby! The queen is coming."

At the thought of the queen's anger, even the little larva fell silent, and all was quiet when the queen appeared.

"Go along," she said to the Maid of Honor and the worker bees. "I want to be alone."

She stood silently for a long time outside the doors of the princesses' rooms, watching them as they slept with their greedy stomachs full .

"Pathetic creatures," she muttered. "Eating and sleeping is all you do from morning to night, getting bigger and fatter. In a few days, you will be mature, and come crawling out of your chambers. Then my days are numbered because I've heard the bees talking to each other about having a younger and more beautiful queen. They think they can shamelessly turn me out, but I won't let that happen. Oh no, my precious little princesses, tomorrow I'll kill all ten of you, and then I can rule here until I die."

With that, she went on her way, but the little larva had heard everything she said and wondered what she ought to do. It was most unfortunate for the little princesses, they were essential for the life of the hive and, as nasty as they had been, it would still be very sad if the evil queen killed them all. She resolved to tell the old Maid of Honor the next time she came by.

When the Maid of Honor appeared later to check on the princesses again, the little larva knocked loudly on her door, but this time the Maid of Honor did not conceal her anger.

"You had better watch out, my precious little larva!" she said, sneeringly. "You are the youngest one of all and create the biggest racket. Next time I'll report you to the queen."

"Oh, this is so important! Please listen!" urged the larva.

"What are you talking about?" asked the old bee, and the little larva explained about the queen's evil plot.

"Heavens, is it true?" cried the Old Maid, her wings knocking together in sheer fright.

"It is and I really think I deserve a little honey for my cooperation," said the little larva. "Then I can lie down and fall asleep with a good conscience."

But her request was ignored, and without waiting to hear any more, the Old Maid left to talk to some the other older bees.

The next evening, when the reigning queen thought all the bees had gone to sleep, she headed over to the princesses' rooms to kill

them. The little larva could hear the queen muttering to herself again, but was so filled with fear, she remained frozen in place.

"If only she would spare the princesses!" the larva thought and inched her way closer to her door to hear what was happening.

Carefully, the queen bee looked all around her and then opened the first princess' door, but that was as far as she got. Immediately, a group of the older, stronger bees were upon her. They swarmed around her from all directions, grabbed her legs and wings, and carried her away.

"What's this!" she screamed. "I am your queen! Are you rebelling?"

"We know, Your Majesty," one of the bees answered, still respectfully, "but we also know you intend to kill the princesses, and there is no way we can allow that. What would happen to us in the fall when it will be your turn to die?"

"Release me," screamed the queen, as she tried to tear herself loose. "I am still the queen and can do as I please. How do you know I will die in the autumn?"

But the bees held on to her tightly and dragged her right out of the hive. Before they released her, she beat her wings in anger, and said to them: "You're nothing but a bunch of unfaithful subjects, not worth ruling over. I won't stay here a moment longer, and I'll go elsewhere and set up a new colony. Who is coming with me?"

Some of the old bees who had been larvae together with the queen declared they would follow her, but there were not many and all the other bees watched as the queen and her faithful few flew away.

"Now we're without a queen," said one the senior bees. "Maid of Honor, we must take good care of the princesses."

Chapter 3

Day after day, they stuffed the princesses full of honey from morning to night. They grew and thrived but they also quarreled constantly among themselves and the bigger they got, the greater the fuss they made. But nobody paid any attention to the little larva.

One morning, the doors to the princesses' rooms were opened, and all ten of them stepped out, now grown-up, beautiful queen bees. The other bees came running up and looked admiringly at them.

"Oh, how lovely they are," the regular bees said. "It's hard to say which of them is the prettiest."

“That’s me,” said one.

“You are mistaken,” said another, and stung the first one.

“You’re all talking nonsense!” shouted a third queen. “I’m more beautiful than any of you.”

Immediately, they were all yelling at each other and soon fought fiercely among themselves. Many of the bees wanted to separate them, but the old Maid of Honor said to let them battle it out.

“We can see who is the strongest of them all; we’ll choose her for our new queen. We can’t have more than one queen, anyway.”

The bees formed a circle and watched the fighting proceed. It lasted a long time, and it was a hard exchange. Wings and legs, bitten off in battle, flew into the air, and eventually, eight of the princesses were dead while the final two were still fighting each other.

One of them had lost its wings; the other had only three legs left.

"The new queen will be a pitiful example no matter who we get," said one bee. "We might as well have kept the old one."

But she could have spared herself that last remark, because just at the same moment, the two remaining princesses stung each other so violently, that they both fell down, stone dead.

"What do we do now?" yelled the bees, as they ran around and in between each other, their legs and wings trembling. "Now, we don't have a queen anymore. What are we going to do? What will happen to us?"

Thoroughly confused, they crawled around in the hive, and didn't know up from down. But the oldest and the wisest bees gathered in a corner and sought each other's advice. For a long time, they went back and forth discussing what they ought to do in this unfortunate circumstance.

Finally, the Maid of Honor spoke up: "If you will follow my advice, I will tell you how to get out of this predicament. A long time ago, I remember a similar incident occurred in the hive. I was a larva myself then, lying in my room and I heard what was happening outside. All the princesses had slaughtered each other, and the old queen had left—exactly like now."

"The bees took one of us larva and put her into one of the princesses rooms. Every day they fed the larva with finest and best honey bread available in the entire hive, and when she grew up, she became a beautiful and serving queen. I remember this so well because I thought they could just as well have selected me. But never mind now; I propose that we carry out this same scheme."

Happily, the bees gave their approval, and wanted to run off immediately to find a larva.

"Wait a minute!" said the Maid of Honor, "it must be one of the youngest larvae because she will need time to think about her new position. When you are born to be a simple worker bee, it isn't so easy to get accustomed to wearing a crown."

The bees thought this too was wise advice, and so the old Maid continued.

"Next to the princesses' rooms, there is a little larva. She is the youngest and smallest of them all, but she must have learned something by listening to the refined conversations of the princesses. I have noticed that she has a good character; it was she who was so honest and told me about the old queen's plot. I propose we choose her."

They all agreed and marched in solemn formation to the narrow, crowded cell where the little larva was lying. Politely, the Maid of Honor knocked on the door, opened it carefully, and told the larva about the decision they had all come to.

In the beginning, she couldn't believe it, but when they carefully carried her into one of the loveliest rooms and fed her as much honey as she could eat, she realized it was true.

"Then I will be the queen!" she said to the Maid of Honor. "You hardly expected that, you old growler!"

"I hope Your Majesty forgets my impolite comments to her from that time. You were lying in an ordinary six-sided cell then," said the old bee, as she curtsied respectfully.

"I forgive you, " replied the new princess. "But, now feed me more honey."

A short time later, the now fully grown queen bee stepped out from her reserved chamber, looking as magnificent and lovely as all the bees could have wished for. And she had learned how to issue orders!

"Get on with your jobs!" she said. "We must increase our supply of honey for the winter, and you youngsters must get busy sweating more wax. I have in mind to build a new section in the hive where the new princesses can live next year. It is not right to have them so close to the common worker larvae."

"Oh, Oh!" the bees said to each other. "You would think she was a designated queen from the egg."

"Not at all!" said the Maid of Honor, "but she had dreams of being a queen, and that is the most important thing."

The Disobedient Owl

Chapter 1

After the morning's rain, it turned into a lovely warm and sunny day, so no one had anything to complain about. Nor were they doing so.

The bees had carried so much pollen to the hive that they were quite exhausted, but still moved from one flower to the next, as happy as the flowers. The butterflies danced in the sunshine, laying their eggs on leaves and stalks, and the dung beetles dragged manure down into the hole where their young ones would develop. The frogs had filled their stomachs with flies and dragonflies, and the baby storks had the last remains of frog legs in their throats. Everywhere it was a peaceful and enjoyable scene after a delightful and busy day, as nature got itself ready for the next cycles of life.

However... four starling youngsters were unhappy, although they were the best-behaved offspring a parent could wish for.

They sat together outside their birdhouse, all of them sulking. It was time for them to go to sleep, but they had other ideas.

They argued that the sun was still shining, and that they weren't sleepy at all. They had practiced their flying and, even though they had caught no flies, they had won praise in the afternoon after they had taken part in fly-snapping exercises; their father said they were coming along. They thought they were big enough now to stay awake until the grown-ups went to bed. And besides, they wanted so much to see the moon.

"Nonsense," said mother starling. "Off to bed with you."

"It's amazing how quickly your youngsters can stand on their own two feet," said the stork, resting up on the roof of a nearby house. "They're ready to fly, and mine still have only down feathers."

"We're not like the fine folks, Your Grace," replied the mother starling respectfully. "As long as it's still summer here, all we get is a lot of fussy kids. As soon as these four go out into the world, I'll lay eggs again, and then it gets crazy once more."

"Hmm!" said the mother stork. "That's not so good. I wouldn't think of asking mister stork to tolerate that situation. I'll speak to your mate about that."

"Oh, please don't do that, Your Grace!" said mother starling, looking downcast. "I'm really delighted with my babies, and it's also the only thing that keeps him here. As long as I have the little ones, he's good. Without them, he'd fly off, and I'd never see him again."

"Oh dear," said the stork.

"Hoot! Hoot!" announced the owl.

"It's the owl!" screamed mother starling. "Get over here, you naughty kids!"

She smacked them with her wings and beak, so they scurried headfirst down into their birdhouse.

"I want to go out and see that owl," declared the boldest of them. The others had the same idea but would not admit it.

“The owl will eat you,” warned mother starling. “It’s a nasty thief. Now close your eyes and be quiet until the sun comes up. Here comes your father, who will sing you a tune.”

Father starling flew in and sat on the branch next to his mate.

“The kids are almost getting to be too much,” she said. “They are flying so far away I can hardly keep track. They won’t go to sleep, they want to see the moon, and now they want to see the owl.”

“Will you behave yourselves!” said father starling looking down at the young ones. “At this time of the day, all nice little birds are asleep. Soon your mother and I will go to sleep too. At night time, decent creatures are not out in the woods. Then it’s full of robbers, bandits, and all kinds of nasty characters.”

And so he piped his evening song as he sat up in the tree above where the mother starling was sleeping with one eye open to be sure no harm came to her youngsters as they slept in the bird house.

Everyone that had been busy during the long, hot day was now sleeping, but some creatures were just waking up, and in a hollow tree nearby, seven closely perched owls were blinking with their round eyes.

“Is it dark enough?” asked one of them.

“Wait a little,” said the oldest and biggest one.

The one who asked, nodded, as did the second, and the third right up to the seventh one. All of them turned their heads first slowly to the right and then to the left as if they were all in agreement. They weren’t, but whatever one of them did, all the others followed.

“Did you hear what the starling said?” asked the oldest owl.

“Yes,” said the six smaller siblings, one after the other.“It’s really a great shame that everyone always talks about us that

way. What do we do differently? All we do is hunt for food for our young and ourselves. We're just like them. We don't need to take that mean-spirited gossip from them. They should be ashamed of themselves."

"Shame, shame, shame, shame, shame, shame," said the other six.

Eventually, it had become as dark as it gets in the light-nights of summer in Denmark. The red sky in the west where the sun went down had vanished, and the stars twinkled across the sky. Under the trees, it was darker, and in the open plains, the moonlight gave everything a white appearance.

"Now it's our time," said the oldest owl.

The six smaller ones flew out of the hollow tree with soft, soundless flaps of their wings, and dispersed around the woods for hunting. But the oldest owl remained, sitting in the tree feeling sorry for himself. He could not forget what the starling had said and was wondering how he could get his revenge. He wanted to prove that he was just as good as the daytime birds.

"Are you sick, owl?" asked a quiet voice close by.

"Who are you?" asked the owl in return.

"I'm just the bat," said the voice. "I've been hanging by my big toe all day long, but now I'm ready to go out, and try to find something to eat."

"You're a robber, a bandit, and a horrible example of riffraff," said the owl. "All decent creatures do their work during the day and sleep at night."

"My goodness, such a moral position," said the bat. "But what's the matter with you? I thought you owls behaved like I do."

"Of course we do, and that means I'm a robber, a bandit, and a horrible example of riffraff," replied the big owl sadly.

He then told the bat what the starling had said, and the bat was in agreement it was a terrible shame to speak about a decent bird like that to one's youngsters. How could the poor kids get on in the world if they were so badly raised?

"What do you care about such silly talk?" said the porcupine that was plodding along under the tree. "I was lying here, and just as I was just waking up, I heard the whole thing. Let's all go about our lives and mind our own business, not caring in the least about those conceited daytime creatures."

"I really think the night is such a poetic time," said the moth that flew by at great speed to avoid being eaten.

"Shucks, I missed that one," complained the bat.

"In the daytime, I can't find my partner at all," said the male glowworm shining among the bushes.

"In the daytime, the farmers are watching the geese," said the fox, licking his chops.

"Well," said the owl. "We're a whole company of fellow-travelers, and naturally, that is comforting, but it is annoying that we have to put up with this at all."

He then flew away to start his hunt, and the others went about their business.

Chapter 2

When the morning sun arose, all the night animals had disappeared as if swallowed up by the earth. The owls and the porcupine, the moth, the bat and the glowworm—there wasn't a trace.

"Such a lovely, lovely forest, and no bandits here!" sang all the young starlings, as they hopped around, practicing their daily chores like cleaning their wings.

The entire woods were teeming with animals, leaping, running and flying, the bright flowers giving off pleasing scents, and the trees delighting in the happiness and contentment felt by all.

But in the evening, when it was time for the starling youngsters to go back into the birdhouse, the boldest of them asked its mother why the owls had become such terrible birds of the night.

"Didn't they have any parents when they were young that could teach them to live like ordinary birds?"

"Let me tell you something, my little one," explained mother starling. "The story goes like this. When the first ever baby owl was little, she was quite a good-natured bird, but she had the problem of being naughty. She would not go to bed at night and even though her mother scolded her for being disobedient, she could not get her little one to behave. The mother owl slept at night and thought all babies had to do the same.

"But when the mother was sleeping, the little one would get up from the nest and sneak out into the dark woods. But then, one night she lost her way, and could not get home. She was so ashamed of her disobedience she vowed never to show her face in the nighttime again."

"But when she went out in the day, wanting to find something to eat, her young feathers made her appear dreadful, the way they hung on her, and all the other pretty birds would be all over her, hacking at her, and mocking her. And so, she went back to going out at night, but all this happened because she would not obey her mother and wouldn't go to bed at night. Now, good night!"

The young starlings thought it was a good story, only they didn't really believe it. They were big enough now so that when someone spoke about 'being nice' or 'being naughty' in a story, they always knew there was something fishy about it and that it was being made up just for them. In the meantime, they became tired and fell asleep.

"Did you hear that" said the bigger owl in the hollow tree. "It's a scandal!"

"Scandal, scandal, scandal, scandal, scandal, scandal!" said the other six owls.

"I've never heard the likes in my life! Why are we mocked and disliked everywhere because we want to eat when it's dark, approaching our prey quietly and modestly as nature intended? I'm sick and tired of it. There's nothing naughty about you young ones going out at night."

"What's all this got to do with the rest of us?" questioned the fox. "The porcupine is right. Let's eat, drink, and be merry. Just fly up to where the young starlings are and hack them to pieces. That will get you revenge on those gossip mongers."

"Well yes, I will eat the young starlings if I can grab them," replied the owl, "but actually I don't really care about getting revenge. What I'd like to know though is why they talk so nastily about us. I suppose the buzzard is a good bird when he eats a mouse during the day, but I'm a nasty bird when I eat a mouse at night. I want to be just as grand and nice as the next bird; I want to be a day bird and go out into the sunshine..."

"Goodness gracious," said the bat. "It's clear you don't have the slightest idea of what you're talking about. I've tried it, you see. The sun shone on me only once—by mistake—and it was horrible."

"I like the sun to shine on me," said the fox. "I mean, when I'm all filled up, and the kids fed. But at night, I need to do my work."

"Oh please, spare me from the sunshine," said the moth, once more passing by. "My nerves can't take it, even to hear the name... sun. I'm happy with nothing more than just a faint moon-glow."

The porcupine shook himself but said nothing. So, they all went back to work except for the old owl that remained sitting for the whole night in a pensive, gloomy mood. When the six others returned before sunrise, the old owl was still sitting; he hadn't budged from the spot.

"You haven't eaten a thing," said the bat.

"I'm thinking about the shame that has come into my life," said the big owl sadly.

"Shame, shame, shame, shame, shame, shame," said the other six owls.

But they were very lucky owls actually because they had stuffed themselves with mice until they were ready to burst. The owl who had sat in the tree had to go to sleep hungry.

The following day, something very strange happened. Life went on in its merry way in the woods, as the flies buzzed, the butterflies danced, and the birds sang, but then... everything suddenly became

still. All the creatures stopped what they were doing, and all was quiet as they stared at an old post in the middle of the meadow.

The old owl sat there, stiff and silent, blinking his eyes crazily in the sunshine he'd never seem. Then, as quickly as things went quiet, there was an enormous commotion.

"The owl! Look at the owl!" screamed a little chaffinch.

"The owl! The owl! The owl!" shouted all the forest's daytime birds. And it was just like when that young and disobedient owl went out in the daytime.

"You Night Thief! You Old Ugly-Puss! You Robber! What are you doing here? See how stupid he looks? See how he blinks those eyes—he's even ashamed of himself! He needs a beating—tear him to pieces! He's a sneak—make him hurt!"

They all attacked the owl at once while he just stood there, blinking his eyes because he could not see in the daylight. The smallest birds hacked at him from the back and the sides, mocking and taunting him. The buzzard circled above his head, screaming along with the others. Even those who were usually enemies forgot their animosities to savage the owl as though he was a threat to the forest.

The owl tried to fly away but could only travel a short distance since he could not see where he was going. He defended himself as best he could, using his beak, claws, and wings, but there were too many of them. Who could imagine there were so many birds in the woods?

"Leave me alone!" he shouted, his feathers all disheveled. "I have done nothing to you. I wanted to go out into the sunshine with you for once. I'm just as good as you. Why are you so horrible?"

"Tear the owl to pieces," screamed the buzzard.

"You of all the birds should be the last to torment me," said the owl as he turned his sad face toward the buzzard, "I'm your flesh and blood cousin. I eat mice at night while you eat mice in the day. Why am I not as good a bird as you?"

"Listen to that disgusting fellow," screamed the father starling. "He wants to be just as good a bird as us. Get him! Get him!"

And so, they attacked again, and the owl quickly realized that he could not defend himself against so many. He lifted his wings and tried to fly away, but he barely moved. At night, he could weave in and out among the tree trunks and branches, but now in the middle of the day, he was bumping into something every moment, hurting himself badly. Sometimes he fell down, amidst cheering rom the other birds. They tore at him, with eathers flying, and he was more dead than alive when he finally slipped into the hollow tree. For a long time, the other birds created a ruckus outside, but they no longer attacked him where he lived.

That evening, before they settled down to sleep, all the birds talked about what had happened, and that included the starlings.

"I told you it would be like that," the mother said.

The youngsters could see that. They lay awake for a long time puzzling over why the owl appeared such a terror at night, but such a pitiful figure in the daytime.

Chapter 3

From that time on, the old owl was a sick bird. He flew out occasionally to catch a mouse, but only enough to keep body and soul together.

"You need to get back on your wings and show your stuff again," urged the porcupine.

"The night is wonderful," squeaked the moth.

"Nighttime is for geese stalking," grinned the fox.

But the owl only shook his head.

"You won't be able to understand it," said the owl, "but I'll get no peace until I can figure it out."

Then there was a strange, refined, and lovely voice that came from the grass that said: "I can explain it, if you'll listen."

"Who are you?" asked the owl.

"I'm the rocket flower who blooms at night," said the voice. "As my flower is so tiny you can't see me, though you can smell me. I come to life at night just like you, and the porcupine, the bat, the moth and all the others. The moth is also my good friend even though it doesn't realize it. It brings my pollen over to my neighbor on the adjoining meadow at the same time it helps itself to my nectar, just like the decorated butterflies and bees do with the attractive flowers that come out in the daytime."

"Well, that's all fine I suppose," said the owl. "You're in the same position I am, and I'd imagine you're despised by the other flowers, as I am despised by the other birds. I don't see how that helps me."

"Yes, it can—because I know why it's that way," said the rocket flower. "I know why we have to operate at night, and there's no shame in that. Now listen."

"Will you do me the favor to wait until my six siblings come back?" asked the owl.

"Gladly," said the rocket flower. "Let them all hear what I have to say, but it has to be before daylight comes. Once the sun rises, I close up, say nothing, and emit no fragrance."

But when the six owls returned home, the sky was already red in the east, and dawn was breaking.

"It's too late now," said the rocket flower, "but there will be time tomorrow."

After they woke up the following evening, the old owl told six the others what the rocket flower had said, and they all agreed they'd speed up their hunt that night, and hurry on home early to hear the story. The fox said he would do the same, along with the moth, the glowworm, and the bat. Even the porcupine wanted to come along.

"I'm so fat I'm a roly-poly," said the porcupine. "If the story is awful enough, maybe I'll slim down."

So, all the night animals rushed through all the hunting chores they had learned as youngsters in order to be there in time to hear the rocket flower's story. And so, long before the sun rose again, there was a strange gathering of animals around the hollow tree as other night animals came too.

They had heard what was going on, but some of them were afraid to show themselves too much. Just like the little wood mouse, who stuck his whiskers up from a hole at the roots of the tree, daring to peek out and listen for as long as the rocket flower's story lasted.

The hare sat crouched, his long ears pointed, ready to spring from under the dock weeds, and the white campion opened its cup-petals just as soon as the sun went down. There were beetles and daddy-longlegs, and many other small animals, more than one would have thought could be out in the nighttime. But many would not show themselves until the owl and the fox, the bat, and the porcupine had solemnly sworn they would leave the smaller ones in peace.

"Agreed," said the old owl. "This matter is important for us as it truly affects our honor as night animals. Even though some of us act as though they couldn't care less, we're all interested in asserting our rights to the day animals. So, let's agree to have total respect among us as long as the rocket flower is speaking."

"Oh, all right then," sighed the fox, "but just as soon as the rocket flower has said its last word, I will eat that little wood mouse over there."

"No, you won't," said the porcupine. "He's mine."

"Actually, I'll want him myself," said the old owl, "that is, if the story gives me any reason to return to my old ways. Oh, the sad times and the sorrows. But, for the moment, let's coexist peacefully and hear what the rocket flower has to say."

The rocket flower emitted a surge of her fragrance and spoke:

"Once last year..."

"Stop!" interrupted the old owl. "We first have to hear where you know all this from so we can be sure you're honest."

"That's what I was about to tell you!" huffed the rocket flower. "It will all come out if you'll just be quiet and open your ears."

"Everybody be quiet," ordered the old owl.

"Wasn't it you that interrupted?" muttered the porcupine.

"It was one evening last year," said the rocket flower. "I was emitting a fragrance, lost in my own thoughts when two humans came walking past me. It was a young man and a young girl, and they were in love. His arm was around her waist, and they both seemed as if food and drink didn't matter to them. At that moment, an owl screamed at them way up in a tree:

"Ugh, that horrible owl!" said the young girl.

"You mustn't say that," insisted her young man. "No animal is horrible. The owl is just as good as that handsome falcon you saw on the picture at home and liked so much," said the man.

"That's a nice young man," observed the owl.

"Oh, be quiet," hissed the porcupine.

"The young girl would not hear of it," continued the rocket flower. "She maintained that the owl was an ugly and treacherous bird. It sneaked around at night, hovering over the little mice and the sweet, young, baby birds. It dared not let its thieving handiwork become common knowledge, but just came flying in silently and then frightened her with its vile screaming."

"I can't figure out why this nice young man would pick her for a girlfriend, the prissy," said the owl.

"Prissy, prissy, prissy, prissy, prissy, prissy," said the other six owls.

"Oh, be quiet," said the bat.

"Then the young man said she must also think the bat is a horrible creature," said the rocket flower.

"Did he mention me?" asked the bat.

"Be quiet," said the owl.

"But the girl wouldn't change her mind about the owl, so he asked her to sit down on the grass; they needed to talk. He spread his raincoat out next to me when they sat down, and he said, 'I can't believe you say things like that. It comes from not understanding nature, and I want to explain it to you so you can see how marvelously all of nature is organized. And then you'll understand when I say no animal is ugly, that they all have a right to live and to thrive as best they can.'"

"Here it comes," said the porcupine.

"Shut up," said the owl.

"Now listen closely," said the rocket flower. "The young man continued speaking in this vein: 'In the old days, the owl was just an ordinary bird-of-prey like the other birds you know, the crow, the eagle, the kite, the buzzard, and the falcon. It didn't have such big round eyes, and it didn't look cross-eyed like it does now. It had short legs, stiff feathers, and hunted during the daytime—just like the other birds.'"

"That must have been a long time ago," suggested the fox.

"It was my great-great-great-great-grandfather," said the old owl.

"Great-great-great-great-great-great," said the other six and they wouldn't stop saying "great-great" until all the animals together told them to be quiet.

"Then it happened one day", continued the rocket flower, "that food was getting scarce. Wherever one owl flew out to hunt, another had already been there. Often, they all had to go hungry in the nest and didn't see how it could end. However, one of them that was smarter than the others and stayed awake at night, while the others were asleep. 'If I go hunting when it's dark, there should be something to find then', he thought. So, he tried it."

"That was my great-great-great..." said the old owl.

"Great-great-great-great-great-great," said the other six.

"Shut up!" shouted all the other animals together. The rocket flower continued the story.

"It really went well for that clever owl, and after a while, he thought all was well enough for him to take a mate. He had also noticed that his stiff feathers made a great commotion when he flew around at night, which amplified every flying-noise making him heard twice as well in the night's stillness. This was a real nuisance, because it warned his frightened prey, and allowed them to get away."

"Terrible," said the old owl.

"Terrible, terrible, terrible, terrible, terrible, terrible," came the echo, which the rocket flower ignored.

"So, when he looked around for a mate among the young females, he had in mind to select one that had the softest feathers possible. She still had to help him with procuring food for the home, but it would be good if the youngsters also had good traits to inherit. He chose the best young mate he could find, and after they lived together, they had four babies in the first year."

"Two of them had inherited their father's stiff feathers," continued the rocket flower, "but the other two had their mother's soft ones. When they finally grew up and went on the hunt themselves, the two of them that had the softer feathers were much cleverer than the other two. They could fly so quietly—can you believe it?—that not a single critter could hear them, and they were on top of the mice in a jiffy. The other two did not fare nearly as well, and one of them died while still young. The other one found a mate, and they had two weak babies, but both perished in the nest."

"That is a strange tale," said the fox.

"Ssh!" said the owl. "I want to hear more."

"Well, one of the soft feathered young owls unexpectedly developed feathers all down his legs. It was such a strange thing that people came from far away to observe it. But when the owl grew up, he was also the cleverest owl that ever existed for night hunting. No matter how fast he traveled, you couldn't hear a sound from him as he flew around. From that day forward, the night hunters that had feathery legs were the most esteemed. They only mated with their own kind, and they took all the food there was so the other owl types eventually died out. It was in the same way with their eyes. Those owls that had the sharpest vision—it was wonderful for them—and they had the most, and the smartest, offspring around. And so, in this way, the owl evolved into what you now see."

Chapter 4

All the night animals were sitting still, listening intently.

"Is there more to the story?" asked the owl, not wanting it to stop.

"Yes," said the rocket flower. "The young girl finally understood all this and promised that she would look more compassionately at all animals. But her boyfriend told her even more."

"Didn't he say anything about me?" inquired the bat.

"Yes, he did," said the rocket flower. "He explained how you evolved in the same way as the owl. Originally you were just an ordinary shrew or something small like that. But then one of your ancestors thought of letting himself drop from a tree or to jump from one branch to another while stretching his legs to get resistance from the air. In this way, the skin was tensed even more.

"Whichever bat tensed its skin the most, and had offspring that could stretch their legs furthest, was the healthiest and most successful of the species. Eventually, offspring appeared that had skin between their legs and bodies, and between their fingers and toes. And in this way, it evolved into the bat we recognize today."

"The more that I think about this, the more I understand it," said the owl. "Is there still more?"

"Yes," said the rocket flower. "The young man spoke at least half the night, and it made me realize why I am what I am. This was because there were so many flowers fighting for the butterflies and bees in the sunshine that one of my ancestors, accidentally kept its petals open at night. And since the variegated petal colors were of no use to it in the dark, where all cats are gray, its petals evolved into being small and inconspicuous. But these petals developed a strong and delightful fragrance so that those whom it wanted to attract, could find it. And things developed in the same way for the moth and the glowworm. They all evolved naturally, and it's all for our benefit."

"That was an excellent story," said the porcupine, "and good for us to realize. But it doesn't really concern me beyond being sure that the night is full of animals I can feed on as my daytime competitors sleep. I'm not really a typical night animal, except that I eat at night and take a little afternoon nap, while the owl and the bat can't do a thing for themselves during the daylight."

"That's just the same for us," said the fox. "Can I ask—is the story over?"

"Yes, I know no more about the subject," said the rocket flower. "Soon, the sun will be up, and then I have to close my petals."

"In that case, permit me..." said the fox leaping at the mouse.

But at the same moment, the porcupine rushed to where the little mouse was sitting.

"Help! Rocket flower! Say something!" screamed the mouse in his distress.

"There is no more," said the rocket flower. "I can tell you how it all makes sense, but I can't change the ways of nature. You should watch out for yourself better, my dear mouse."

The porcupine joyfully squashed the poor mouse between its teeth, but the fox was furious.

"You thief! You scoundrel," he screamed. "Now I will eat you!"

"Be careful you don't choke on me," laughed the porcupine rolling himself into a ball with all of his quills erect.

"I know your system, and I can overcome it," said the fox.

So, he rolled the porcupine away by pushing at him with his paw. It hurt, but the fox was angry and wanted revenge. He kept on pushing until he reached a little wood pond and with splash, in rolled the porcupine. He had to unravel himself so as not to drown, and the fox bit sunk his teeth into the porcupine's neck.

As soon as the sun came up, all seven owls were sitting on a branch of the hollow tree, swaying and nodding their heads with amusement as they thought about the story. The bat was also hanging contentedly by his big toe, thinking he was a young bachelor again.

"It's great," said the old owl.

"Great, great, great, great, great, great," said the other six.

"Now I won't worry myself over what the starlings say," said the old owl. "The youngsters talk according to their understanding, and their parents know no better. That story about the disobedient owl was not as good as the rocket flower's."

"Humans aren't any smarter," said the bat.

“That young man was smart,” said the old owl. “I’ll give him credit for that. There’s only one thing I wish he had explained to that girl. You know what those dummies say about me—that I can predict the weather? They say when I utter: ‘Hoot, Hoot!’ the weather will turn bad, and when I say: ‘T-wit!’ the weather will be nice. But it’s my mate that says ‘t-wit’ and I say ‘hoot, hoot’! Ha! Ha!”

“Ha! Ha! Ha! Ha! Ha! Ha!” laughed the other six.

“Rocket flower,” said the owl, “good little rocket flower, can you tell me if the young man knew the difference, or was he also just as dumb as the others?”

But the rocket flower had already folded up her cup-petals, bent her head down under a heavy dewdrop, and didn’t answer.

“Good morning!” said the sun behind the beach’s edge.

“Good morning!” said the starling and the finch and everything else freshly awakened to the new day.

“Good night!” said the old owl.

“Night, night, night, night, night, night!” repeated the other six.

The Man Who Wouldn't Eat Strawberries

Chapter 1

Once upon a time, there was a man so decent that he couldn't stand to live in this world. No matter where he went, he saw nothing but quarreling, and people opposing one another. Everyone only looked after what belonged to them and treated their neighbors unfairly. Governments made war against each other, people fought each other and always seemed to be at each other's throats. Nobody helped anybody; nobody forgave anybody.

Finally, tired of this, he settled down in a faraway place in the countryside to have as little contact with people as possible. He found a wonderful house, miles from anywhere, in a spruce grove right by the sea. He rented it from the farmer that owned it and moved in right away. Now he would sit and smoke his pipe by the beach, looking out at the ocean and believing wickedness and cruelty wouldn't wound his good heart anymore.

Whenever he ventured out to spend his days by the sea, he took a picnic with him; he was especially fond of ham. He would buy a large, cured, ready-to-eat joint from the farmer, and kept it in his

cool, dark cellar. One morning, he ventured down the stairs, but the ham was gone. Well, actually, the bone was still lying there, but nothing else, and when he looked around, he saw the tail of a mouse disappearing into a hole.

"Well, I can't have that!" said the man to himself, and he hurried over to the farmer's house. When he got there, he found who he was looking for; at the gate sat the farmer's purring cat. He greeted the cat and said:

"Now listen, cat, there is a mouse in my cellar."

"Ah," said the cat knowingly.

"Will you eat it for me?"

"It would be a pleasure" replied the cat. So, the cat went over to the little house, and it didn't take long before he caught the mouse and devoured it in only two bites, including the tail.

"Thanks," said the man.

"It was a trifle," said the cat.

The next morning the man went for a walk in a grove of firs and went over to a bird's nest that rested a bit off the ground.

He wanted to look at the three delightful and tiny yellow finch nestlings he knew would be inside. He had often watched them at a safe distance so that the mother bird wouldn't get frightened and fly away, perhaps even abandoning her babies. When he now approached the nest, it was empty.

He presumed that some accident must have befallen them because the nestlings were far from ready to fly away. The mother yellow finch was sitting at the top of the spruce tree crying miserably, and just as the man was about to console her, he noticed the farmer's purring cat sitting on the fence.

"Now listen, cat," he said. "Yesterday there were three young ones in the nest."

"Indeed," said the cat.

"You've eaten them?"

"Of course," came the cat's response.

"Then I will have to punish you."

"Nonsense," replied the cat.

The man picked up a stone and threw it, but it missed the cat. In a flash, the cat raced up a tree and sat there, grinning at the man.

"I can't tell you how much your behavior upsets me," said the man. "I've moved out here to be at peace and to be among nature's beauty. I've come here to get away from all the human evil and cruelty, and then I meet a devil like you. You don't have a heart in you, since you were cruel to the small, innocent nestlings that had just come into the world, and upset their mother when she was so happy. Have you no feelings of honor either? What is a supposedly wise old cat doing murdering three tiny nestlings?"

He grabbed a stone and threw it at the cat again but missed it. The cat climbed up higher in the tree.

"Stop throwing stones at me," it said. "You could get lucky and hit me. Sit down on the fence, and I'll tell you something."

"If you have something to say to excuse yourself and apologize, I'd be happy to listen," said the man.

"I don't intend to excuse myself at all," said the cat. "I have done nothing other than what nature intended for me. On the contrary, I'd like to set you straight, you hypocrite."

"I beg your pardon?" said the man sitting down on the fence.

"So, you're supposed to be a good man, in love with the entire world, and yet yesterday, you came strolling over to the farm, asking me to gobble up the mouse in the cellar. You thought I was a splendid cat, a good cat, exactly like a cat should be. When I finished the work you asked me to do, you patted me and praised me. I never thought of myself for a minute as a bad cat. Then today, you call me horrible names and try to hurt me because I gobbled up three snotty nestlings."

"The mouse had eaten my ham," said the man indignantly.

"So, you said, but dare I ask you what you had for dinner yesterday?"

"Well... I cooked a chicken."

"Yes," replied the cat. "I heard you order it from the farmer and saw with my own eyes when the girl there chopped its head off. So, can you tell me whether that chicken had eaten your ham, or done you harm in some other way?"

"Well, no..." said the man thoughtfully.

"You jerk!" sneered the cat.

The man was so shocked at being spoken to that way he dropped the stone he intended to fling at the cat. Instead, he sat with his hand under his chin and thought about what the cat had said.

"Maybe you can kindly tell me," continued the cat, "where the ham that should have gone into your stomach—but ended up in the mouse's—came from?"

"It was from a pig" answered the man.

"So it was, and I knew pig well. It lived over at the farm, grunting as it fed, but harmed no one. I also watched it being slaughtered. Dare I inquire honestly of you: What bad thing did the pig do to make you want to eat it so much?"

"Well...," said the man quietly, now realizing what the cat was telling him with all its questions.

"So, there you go," said the cat. "You praised me when I ate the mouse but scolded me when I ate the nestlings. I was hungry. It didn't bother your conscience to eat the pig and chicken because you were hungry. You're a human being who thinks he's smarter than all the other creatures; you think you can live by different standards?"

Chapter 2

The man saw he could not explain himself to the cat, so he went home to his house, sat down, and began speculating. And now he was even more upset. It had been horrible to see the yellow

mother finch wailing for her lost nestlings at the top of the fir tree, but the chicken also had a mother that was now weeping over her loss. And maybe the mouse had small young ones that were now dying of hunger since no one was there to look after them. Even the pig may have left a weeping family behind.

The man became sick in his good heart thinking about it, and after going over it for a while, stood up, slammed the table, and announced:

"I will never eat meat again!"

But so much distress and consideration had made him exceptionally hungry. So, he went down to his garden to get a handful of lettuce and radishes. As he bent down, and already had his hand on a couple of delicious-looking lettuce plants, he heard a voice yelling:

"Oh, God! Oh, God! Am I going to die?"

The man fell backwards and stared terror-stricken at the lettuce.

"Are you alive, too?" he asked.

"And why shouldn't I be alive?" said the lettuce. "Is it because I don't fly around like a bird, or run around like a mouse or mew like a cat? Can't you see I am growing and thriving? I eat with the help of my roots just like you eat with your mouth, and my food gets digested in my leaves just like in your stomach. I look forward to the sun just as much as you and the birds. If I have permission to live, I'll have flowers and then seeds, and they will make some baby lettuce. But now I must prepare to die."

"Not a chance," said the man. "Not for anything in this world, would I hurt you. I'll just have radishes instead."

He hurried over to the radish bed and pulled up a big one.

"Oh, woe is me!" sighed the radish, and died on the spot.

The man dropped it and let out a scream.

"Were you living, too?"

The radish couldn't answer him because it was dead. But one of the other radishes standing alongside in the bed answered instead.

"Of course we are living," it said. "What else? But we know that we will die. We are just planted and raised for the pleasure of people's stomachs. Humans are just awful gluttons who never think of anything except food and eating up everything that comes even near them. Worse thieves and murderers you can't find in the entire world."

"I am not a thief or a murderer," rebutted the man. "I won't eat you. I'll satisfy my hunger by eating a few strawberries."

"Of course," said the radish. "Even more murder. Do you think, you silly man, that strawberries don't have a life, too?"

The man ran from the garden, sat in his house, and cried. When his housekeeper Anna tried to give him a bowl of strawberries from the garden, he sent her away, but as soon as she'd gone, he thought he would die of hunger unless he was ready to become a murderer—but his good heart would never let him be one again. When he didn't die immediately, but got hungrier and hungrier, he went to his pantry and grabbed a delicious-looking, red apple he had been saving.

"This is mine to eat, now," he said. But hardly had he set his teeth into it before the apple sighed deeply and sadly.

"Oh, dear," it said. "I knew this was coming as soon as that murderer tore me off the tree. Now he'll eat me and throw my core into the trash can instead of onto the nice, rich soil. There will be no small apple trees coming from me."

The man dropped the apple onto the floor and stared at it as it rolled under the table. Then he looked up towards a noise over by the open window, and there was the cat that had jumped onto the window ledge. It sat there, comfortable enough, with its tail curled around its paws, and with its devious eyes, stared at the man.

"Well," it said. "How is it going? Did you find something to eat?"

"No!" groaned the man.

"You jerk!" shouted the cat.

"I don't have the strength to hurl something at you," sighed the man.

"No?" said the cat. "You don't. And soon you'll die of hunger. You're the biggest fool who ever walked the earth. What are you speculating so foolishly about? Live as nature designed you. Take care of your nutritional needs and let others take care of theirs. The mouse eats the ham when it gets the chance, and the cat eats the mouse when it can grab hold. Life is full of conflict and struggle, nothing else."

The man gazed at the cat for a moment.

Then he jumped up, opened the kitchen door, and yelled out for his housekeeper:

"Anna! Hurry up and make me some lunch, I'm dying of hunger. I want lettuce and radishes with a piece of that new ham, and then more of that chicken. Then I'll have that huge bowl of strawberries. Hurry, Anna!"

Because he was so hungry, while Anna made his meal, he picked up the apple from the floor and ate it in three mouthfuls. Then he threw the apple core at the cat and hit it smack on the nose which made it sneeze and leave in a big hurry.

"Take that, you jerk," said the man.

Why The Worms Left

Chapter 1

There was a place in the forest called Beech Hill because the tallest and straightest beech trees grew there. They stood so tall that the ships in the ocean used the hill as a beacon. All around the countryside, you could see their verdant crowns. Every evening, the raven sat in the tallest of the trees thinking things over, peering far out over the landscape.

But the raven was not the only one peering far out; the trees, too, looked to the distance and were the loveliest sight in the forest. Everything that lived on Beech Hill was beautiful, strong and tall; there was no comparison.

When the forester's son needed worms for fishing, he went to Beech Hill, for the earthworms there were the fattest and biggest. When the forester's daughter needed some good soil for starting her roses, she went to Beech Hill, because there the ground was rich and black. And when a young guy wanted to make a bouquet to impress a special girl, he could find them at Beech Hill, because there the anemones were the whitest, the lilies-of-the-valley had the sweetest fragrance, and the wild roses on the fence in the foothills were more beautiful than anywhere else in the woods.

Each autumn, the cranes arrived from far away to have a party among the red hips on the rose bushes. That's how it was for the flies, the bees, and the butterflies, too; they were all so beautiful. If a large and beautiful chaffinch sat and sang somewhere in the forest, then all the other birds knew immediately the sound came from Beech Hill. If a lovely new sapling emerged from the ground, the other trees presumed it had begun life from a seed stuck on the fur of a fox or a hare that had been on Beech Hill.

All those living there understood this and were proud of it, and everyone embraced each other like they belonged to a large family. Aside perhaps from the natural food chains, that is! True enough, the chaffinch ate the flies and earthworms when it could find them; the fox preyed on the chaffinch nestlings; the trees competed for sunshine, and the flowers for the bees, just like everywhere else in the world. But whoever was fed upon and died, they accepted it with dignity.

"It stays in the family," they said.

And the overall forest was proud of Beech Hill because it shared precious space. The other trees, clustered around the foothills, were delighted with the shelter provided against storms and the cold. They all felt that if everything went well for Beech Hill, then everything went well for the forest, too; it was like waving a celebratory banner for all.

When spring arrived, you couldn't mistake it; there was such a commotion and a longing in the air on the hill. Birds sang out, and those who couldn't sing, hummed, whistled, sighed, and bubbled over with joy, as though their hearts would burst. The sun moved across the sky in all its radiance, and those that paid attention, could hear it saying:

I'm shining, I'm shining, come out, come out!
All you who are yearning, still covered by ground,
All you who suffered through the dark winter's cold,
Burst out, little bud, break out from your cover,
I'm shining, I'm shining, come out, come out!

When it rained—and it always did so on schedule for everyone—the words heard were:

I'm dripping, I'm dripping, come out and grow up,
Seed in the hill and leaf at the top,
All you green buds and burgeoning flowers,
All of you waking from a deep winter's sleep,
I'm dripping, I'm dripping, come out and grow up!

Those on whom it rained and shined understood what was happening and did what they could. There were discussions each night in the beech tree's buds on whether to break out. Down on the ground, the anemones sang with their subdued and delicate voices:

We're lying and longing in the earth's black soil,
Only rarely do we see the bright golden sun,
Rain, drip again, and sun, shine upon us once more,
So, we too feel spring's welcome,
And the warm days to come.

And then it came for the anemones and one morning, the sunrise in the east shone straight into their thousands of white petal cups.

"Lift your heads!" said the sun. "You are my favorite flowers. My warming rays will wake you up and release you from your black cover. From me you have life, without me, you will die. Hurry while you have me."

The anemones straightened up, as the sun requested, and by noon they were as erect as a regiment of soldiers. As the sun was sinking in the west, they all followed it with bowed heads, but the next morning, they were bending toward the east, where the sun was rising, and they did the same thing every day.

Then the beech themselves sprung out, and every leaf unfolded so it cast a shadow over the anemones. Finally, not a single sunbeam could penetrate the canopy causing the anemones to die. Obediently, they withered, but not before sprinkling their seeds on the ground, so that their offspring could also live cheerfully in the sunshine the next year.

Chapter 2

As summer passed, no one missed the anemones. Fragrant lilies-of-the-valley and all kinds of other flowers sprouted and everybody on Beech Hill was busy, adapting to survive, but remaining content. Everywhere there were crowds and swarms, singing and chatting right until the evening, when tired, they settled down and became quiet.

"I wonder why those of us on Beech Hill are the best there is in the forest?" wondered the chaffinch one evening. It could not sleep because the moon was shining so brightly, and the nightingale was singing in the thicket at the foothills of the Hill. The song stopped briefly when a moth danced right in front of the nightingale's beak, but it missed the chance to catch it.

"It's because we live so high up," said the oldest beech. "The sunshine and rain arrive here first before the others get any, and so we get the best of it."

"It's because we are from such a distinguished family," said the wild rose. "Year after year, we've kept to ourselves and don't get mixed up with the riff-raff."

"It's because we are so smart," said a large bumblebee. "All smart creatures get by."

"Actually, it's because of the black humus on the forest floor," announced the raven in its hoarse voice, before it beat its wings and flew away.

"Oh, he's quite the expert," sneered the chaffinch. "He says something enormously profound that nobody understands and then flies away without explaining it."

"How can it be that I owe my beauty to the ugly black humus?" questioned the wild rose snobbishly.

"What's the humus got to do with me?" asked the chaffinch.

"The raven is crazy," said the bumblebee. "Why should a load of soil be so special?"

"Well, let's ask the black humus," suggested the beech.

Bending its branches deeply and touching the ground, the beech inquired:

"Hey, black humus... tell us if we owe all our happiness to you?"

Everybody listened carefully, but the humus said nothing. The beech asked again, as did the chaffinch, the bumblebee, and the lily-of-the-valley.

Finally, the humus replied: “Leave me alone.”

And they couldn’t get a word more out of the humus, no matter how much they tried. Then morning came, and they had other things to think about. But the next evening, they talked about it again—without success. Just before the raven flapped its wings and flew away, it screeched:

“It’s because of the black humus!”

And so, all the questioning began again.

“Why are you bothering me so much? Why are you asking me all these questions?” said the humus, finally replying. “You’re all doing well, so don’t trouble yourselves about the rest. I have my secrets, and I’ll keep them to myself. I’m full of secrets and you don’t understand how they tingle, crawl, and expand in me. It’s shocking if you knew what I know.

"You know nothing," said the chaffinch, and all the others agreed.

As the moon shone on them next to the oldest beech where the chaffinch sat, a little, brightly illuminated spot appeared just as an earthworm was coming out of the ground. "What a delicious-looking worm," said the chaffinch. "If I weren't so sleepy, I'd eat it."

"I wouldn't do that," advised the black humus. "Stay with flies—they'll serve you better."

"What is that supposed to mean?" asked the chaffinch. "Maybe it's the earthworm that makes Beech Hill so lovely?" it said sarcastically.

"Maybe," replied the humus dryly.

The chaffinch almost keeled over with laughter, as did the beech, along with the bumblebee and the wild rose, which laughed so hard its leaves almost fell off too early. All around the forest, even the others not fortunate enough to live on the Hill giggled uproariously.

Chapter 3

When the fall arrived, the forester felled a lot of trees, leaving the stumps behind, but touched none that grew on Beech Hill.

"Beech Hill will stand just as it is for as long as I live," said the forester to his workers as they rested with their axes. "It's the most beautiful part of the forest," he added, and the men nodded in agreement, but little did they know that something was going to happen.

That spring, Beech Hill stood almost too proud and green, and visible over the whole countryside. However, with only stumps around, many birds had to build their nests elsewhere, away from the forest, and all kinds of ferns grew up in the empty spaces around the tree stumps.

"I'm not sure about things this year," observed the black humus. "Is our glorious era ending?"

"Maybe the earthworm isn't feeling well!" teased the chaffinch.

"Maybe," said the humus quietly, and everybody laughed so hard it echoed in the forest. But the humus didn't laugh and then things began to change.

"There aren't enough rose hips here to fill us up," complained the thrushes.

"It's tough in this autumn cold weather," said the chaffinch. "It would be nice to be a migrating bird."

"It will get worse in years to come," said the black humus.

"Oh?" said the chaffinch. "Maybe the earthworm isn't favoring us any longer?"

"Maybe," replied the humus.

They all laughed again, but this time the laughter sounded hollow. Probably no one believed the humus, but they could see things were not as good as before, and concern grew widely about the future.

When spring next arrived, and the anemones burst forth, the sun was not pleased.

"There aren't as many of you," the sun said. "Not as tall either and not even so pretty. What's wrong with you?"

"We don't know," replied the anemones. "We don't understand it, we do what we can, but the ground is still so cold this year."

"My crown doesn't feel as filled out as usual," said the old beech as it was budding.

"There aren't as many lilies-of-the-valley this year on Beech Hill," said the forester's daughter.

And as the years passed, things got much worse. Ten years passed, then twenty, then forty. The flowers died and new shoots emerged from seeds. The new chaffinches continued in their old ways, the beech was still standing, and the same raven was sitting at the top. But everything had changed.

Those living at Beech Hill felt that life had become hard and difficult. They felt that spring was coming later, and that summer didn't last as long. In the fall, the storms were worse, and the winters more bitter cold. The flowers didn't have their usual fragrance, and the birds didn't sing as sweetly. The beech tree's crown was thinning, displaying a lot of dead branches. There were no lilies-of-the-valley anymore, and the wild roses had become so tiny, no one noticed them.

"What's happening here?" wondered the oldest beech, perplexed. "Are we all going to perish? We are still so young and beautiful. What have we done wrong? Who is destroying us?"

"It's the black humus!" squawked the raven, flying away.

"The black humus?" said the beech, now quite confused. "Wasn't it the humus that allowed us to prosper? So how come it's now the humus that is destroying us? Humus! Humus! Explain yourself! Defend yourself! We are dying; we will not make it!"

"Do you think I'm any better off?" replied the humus. "Just like all of you, I'm not my old self anymore. I'm angry and going downhill and will become even more bitter and more useless as the years pass. I'll become hard and disgustingly lumpy, and believe me, death will be everywhere on Beech Hill."

"So, let's try to fight it!" urged the beech. "What do you know about our misery? Why is the raven always calling out your name? For once, is it true what he is saying? Please speak up and help us."

"The raven isn't any cleverer than you," replied the humus. "It knows a little about this and that, but not where it is all heading. I know all there is, but I won't say anything. It wouldn't help in the slightest to talk about it. You won't believe anything I say. Fate is upon us... we're all going to die."

"Maybe it's the earthworm?" asked the chaffinch, now in a more serious tone.

"Maybe," replied the humus.

"Oh, what's the point of going on like this?" said the old beech angrily. "I don't think it's time to talk nonsense. I know the earthworm, a decent fellow that crawls in the ground between my roots, but how could a small creature like that have anything to do with the glorious green crown I had in the old days? Is it causing my present miserable state?"

"It doesn't harm you or help you," said the humus. "It is just what it is."

"Should I be grateful to that miserable worm for my red hips?" asked the wild rose indignantly.

"And should I be grateful, too, because my family is the most distinguished in the forest?" questioned the chaffinch.

"When we're finally ready to die, I'll tell you all about it," said the black humus and would say no more.

Chapter 4

As more time passed, things got continually worse. The proud beeches were rotting inside, and then just collapsed. Large, gray ferns were growing where previously there were anemones. The wild rose in the fence died. The heather expanded up the hillside and filled the whole space with its tough, brown twigs.

"It's like living on a poor farm," said the chaffinch. "It's just like the story I heard when I was in the nest, that the loveliness of Beech Hill was only make-believe."

"What in the world is up with Beech Hill?" said the new forester. The old one had retired and moved away.

The time had come when everyone could see that life was all but over on Beech Hill. All the trees had fallen, except for the oldest.

It was just a withered old tree trunk with a few green twigs at the top. Every time the wind blew, the tree groaned and rumbled, and another old, dead branch fell off.

That spring, only one tiny anemone crept out from down in the heather and the bumblebees never came before the heather was flowering; there was nothing else for them. The chaffinch had moved to another area in the forest, and the raven had died.

From the countryside, you couldn't see Beech Hill at all anymore, because there were no trees left, and the ships had chosen

another beacon for sighting land. The new forester shrugged his shoulders and left to work elsewhere because there was nothing to do. Nothing would grow anymore on the hill, and it lay there like an ugly, dead eyesore in the forest.

"Beech tree... old beech tree... are you still alive?" asked the black humus.

"Barely," replied the beech. "I have seven green leaves left because of my age, and before the year is out, I'm finished."

"Me, too," said the humus.

"Oh, really?" inquired the beech.

"I'm only left with raw sub-soil," said the black humus, "if you know what that is."

"No, I don't know about that, but I'm past caring about what's going on within us. We're finished... that's all."

"Sure," said the humus. "That's all, and now I will tell you how it happened."

"It's more fun to be alive than listening to stories," said the beech. "But at our age, we have to be content just to see time go by."

"Bend down a little," said the humus. "I'm almost unable to speak... there is just so little remaining of me, you understand?"

"But I can't bend down," said the beech, "and I have no branches to lower down towards you except some twigs up on top."

"Well..." said the humus, "now someone is coming that can tell the story better than I can."

"I don't see anybody," said the beech.

But at the foot of the beech tree, there was a thin, little earthworm that was barely moving. It was pale and appeared most unhappy.

"It's just a pathetic looking earthworm," said the humus.

"Will that miserable earthworm reveal what has happened?" asked the beech. "I've heard nothing so crazy in the four hundred years I've lived on the Hill. I never thought I'd hear anything sensible from a pathetic worm."

"Tell the beech all about it, little earthworm," urged the humus.

But the earthworm was twisting itself horribly, trying to bore down into the ground.

"I have nothing to say," said the earthworm. "I only want to fi nd a leaf I can take down into the ground with me, but there probably aren't any here. I might just as well die like the rest of my family."

"Death and misery everywhere," said the beech. "I've only got seven leaves and I can't spare any of them. It's not very much for a beech of my age. In the old days, I had plenty of frills. Then

I would gladly sprinkle so many leaves over you that you'd be drowning in them."

"Heavens," said the earthworm respectfully. "It never would occur to lift my eyes up to green leaves. It's only when one falls down, lies there withering... if I am not insulting anyone by saying that..."

"Oh no, little earthworm," said the humus sighing. "You have insulted nobody. You do not understand what you have meant to Beech Hill. The beech doesn't understand, and no one knows except me... you worked with me while we all prospered. But now it will be obvious to everyone, we all are no more."

"I'd better get back," said the earthworm, but before it could go any further, a visiting chaffinch snapped it up, and flew with it back to the nest in another part of the forest. This was its ways, learned from its upbringing and its ancestors who have prospered on Beech Hill.

"Now we two are the only ones living," said the humus, "but our time is now very limited. Our last hope for life disappeared with the earthworm."

"I don't understand," said the old beech. "But please tell me about it, if you can."

"Well, I'll try if I can last that long," said the humus. "I'll tell you the story of Beech Hill, but my voice may only reach the tops of the nasty heather brush."

"It'll be all right," replied the beech. "If I miss something, I'll figure it out, anyway. It is my story, and I ought to know about it."

"Actually, you damned well should!" said the humus, momentarily angry, but then it sighed and began the story.

"It's true what the raven said, that such amazing things sprang up from me, out of the black humus. Every spring the anemones and the lilies-of-the-valley, and all the other plants showed themselves from deep inside me. I sent juicy nutrients up through your roots so that your leaves became green and broad. You don't deny that, do you?"

"At my age, one denies nothing," said the beech.

"Good," said the humus. "But now the question is: Where did I get all my stuff from?"

And, while it was far too late, realization dawned on the old beech.

"Oh dear, I'm thinking we gave back to you what we received. I know that every year my leaves fell down on you, or a twig I had no use for. I'd let that tumble down to you, too. My branches, broken off by a storm, were also yours. My fruits fell right into your lap."

"Go on," urged the humus, relieved that the beech was doing most of the talking.

"I think you got it all back, but you did well with it, and thanks for the help. Heavens, I would never have believed it was in better condition than when I'd got it."

"That's right," confirmed the humus. "You returned all that you got. The anemones, the lily-of-the-valley, the wild rose, they all came again. The flies died, and they fell on me and even things from the chaffinch—there isn't a feather or a piece of eggshell that didn't land in its proper place. But have you never considered how I delivered new things every spring when I got nothing but used things in the fall?"

"I haven't," said the beech. "I never thought about it. I was tall and green and beautiful; the sun shone on me, the rain fell on me, and the birds sang in my branches. Why should I speculate about anything? I was living so well."

"Well, I have always been speculating," said the humus huffily. "Perhaps I'm more profound than you are and there weren't so many things that disturbed me. Although things crawled into me a lot, it was deep down in the darkness. I saw none of the activity, but listened, and thought even more. I never completely understood it, and I can't tell you what forces were working in me, but I was like a workshop, a factory that never shuts down. But not anymore."

"Really?" asked the beech. "So, what have you been able to work out?"

"My thoughts are," replied the humus, "that inside me the withering leaves were being converted into wonderful juices which rose in you, making you a splendid example. It needed rain and a little sunshine... well, it seemed like the biting cold and freezes did some good, too. Everything sizzled and bubbled in me because you use an incredible amount of my juice up there, but directing everything... that was the earthworm."

"I can't understand that," said the beech. "Are you sure?"

"Of this, I am," answered the humus. "First, at night when everything was quiet, and the chaffinch was sleeping, the earthworms came up, grabbed a leaf and dragged it around. Their intention was to pull it into the ground, but often they didn't finish that night because they are tiny and weak creatures. So, the leaf remained wrapped on the surface until it got dark and quiet again, but all the time it was changing. Later, the worms ingested the half-rotten leaf, and it went straight through their long bodies, coming out as a kind of loose soil."

"Remarkable," said the beech. "That's the way the earthworm makes you, but what about my twigs and branches?"

"That's the way it happened," said the black humus. "Your twigs would rot in the rain and then the earthworm would eat those too, bit by bit. But it did more than that. It dug tunnels across and diagonally, up and down and everywhere inside me, and water and air ran through these tunnels to make me good and healthy black humus. And in these tunnels, your fine roots moved around and settled, ready to expand."

"It's getting weirder and weirder," said the beech. "My delicate roots... do you know the most delicate of them are the most important?"

"I do indeed," replied the humus, glad the lesson was sinking in.

"Without them, I can't make it. If they break off from me, the root attached to them dies. It's those little roots that give me life."

"I know that too," said the humus, "because it's me they are sucking on."

"And I owed that to the earthworm?" acknowledged the beech, finally understanding. "You did," said the humus. "But we owe it even more.

It's the earthworm that plowed and harrowed me, it crushed me and exchanged me, turned me, and moved me—all the same things that people do with their machines and equipment— that's what the poor, little earthworm does by merely twisting and meandering around in the ground."

"Wonderful," said the beech, forgetting for a moment it was dying. Then the old tree was quiet for a moment, and so was the humus, for it too was old and tired of all that chatting.

But then the humus whispered: "That's why we owed our magnificent lives to the earthworms. We are all indebted to them since it was they who made Beech Hill so beautiful, praised over the whole countryside. Then the old beech shook itself, and three new leaves fell from the stem.

"Earthworms!" it yelled. "I want earthworms!"

But nothing happened.

"You're too late," said the humus sadly, "they have left and will never come back. The chaffinch just gobbled up the last one."

"Why did they go away?" asked the beech.

"It wasn't a good place for them any longer," replied the humus. "It all began when they chopped down the trees at the bottom of the Hill. Then there was too much cold and stormy weather, and way too much sun. I spoke to the earthworms about it, and they had to crawl away, they said, or they'd surely die. It was too hot and then too cold."

"Bah!" retorted the beech. "Can those creeping things make such demands on us? I've been standing here for hundreds of years through frost and sunshine, to the glory of the whole forest and never whined once. Then, in our old age, we have to put up with those good-for-nothing creepies demanding they are given so much respect everywhere."

"You talk as though you still have influence," said the humus. "And what have you got to complain about with the earthworms?

They didn't chop the trees down! They did their work quietly and diligently with nothing more than a murky life in the ground. No one ever invited them when you had a spring party; everyone held them in contempt apart from those who ate them. No one ever gave them the credit they deserve. Now they're gone, and we're hurting."

"We want them back," said the beech.

"But that's impossible," said the humus. "Don't you think I've done my best to keep them here? What was I before, and what am I now? The couple of leaves I still have inside me are only halfway converted to more humus because there are no earthworms around. The fallen leaves are lying all matted up like a hard cake, and the roots of the heather and the grasses are weaving themselves through them. It's just unfinished humus! Don't, you see? Just disgusting peat, like the stuff lying in the bog, a cemetery for our once green and joyful life. Nothing can grow anymore except heather, heather, and more heather. And it will get worse soon. The sand and the hardpan will slide under the heather and will become hard as a rock. Then it really will be over for Beech Hill, and we'll all be dead."

"That's nice to hear," said the beech. "A lovely story when you're standing with one foot in the grave and no more than a few leaves still on your crown. That pesky earthworm!"

"That's the way it goes," said the humus. "Who of us thinks about anything in the best-of-times? What do we know about where anything comes from, and to whom we owe anything? Let's be humble."

"Let's scream, be defiant and protest!" urged the beech. "If you're accustomed to getting down on your knees in front of all of us, okay, but I'm used to holding my head up high. For centuries, you could see me far out on the surging seas. Is a lowly worm now going to squash me? I'll yell until my last breath, so everyone over the whole forest can hear it: the earthworm must come back and do its duty."

"You old fool," said the humus, and never spoke again.

The beech continued to shake and scream, demanding the return of the earthworm, but no one heard it over twenty feet away.

"Earthworm! Earthworm! Earthworm!"

Then the last leaves fell off, and it was all over. For a long time, the old beech remained high on the hill, but merely as a sad, dead stump. But now they call the place: Heather Hill

The Coral That Built An Island

Chapter 1

This story begins a long time ago, out in the ocean—the real, unimaginably deep waters that are so immense ships can travel for many days without seeing land. It happened in the tropical oceans close to the surface with the sun shining, where the water is almost as warm as a hot bath. But in the depths, it's as cold as ice and darker than the blackest night.

The ocean doesn't have the same depth everywhere because at the bottom, there are tall mountains and nestling valleys just like on land. And there was one place where the tallest of mountains jutted right up from the bottom close to the surface. If you stood on top of it, from every angle you wouldn't see anything but water, water, and more water. But deep down there was so much more to look at.

On the submerged mountain sides, enormous amounts of seaweed were growing, stretching a mile wide up and down the steep slopes. When the waves rolled in, the seaweed fluttered in the water, just like leaves on trees up on land flicker in the wind. But the seaweeds' main stems were not nearly so dense and stiff as the beech and oak trunks, so they wafted back and forth, wherever the waves and currents nudged them.

The seaweed stems were taller than any tree on land, but they never grew above the ocean's surface. This was because when their leaves touched the air, they dried out and withered. But when the water was quiet, they spread out, shining with magnificent colors, reds, yellows, greens, and browns, just like the autumn foliage in the woods.

Between the crowns of the seaweed stands, shoals of lively fish swam from one plant to the other just like birds flying in the woods. But these were not some uninteresting gray fellows like cod and pike and eels. Many of them glistened like gold and silver, one was sky blue, another scarlet red. There was the porcupine fish which could inflate itself like a ball and throw its quills out to all sides, creating terrible fear in the other animals. There were many animals in the seaweed habitat.

There were mussels with their strange shells, and there were snails with large, decorated shells. There were octopuses, which came rushing backwards through the water at unbelievable speed. There were large crayfish, also swimming backwards, cutting things with their pincers, and flat, lopsided crabs crawling sideways, yet always advancing. Sometimes hordes of several hundred large, clumsy sea turtles were foraging in the seaweed just like cows in the pasture.

It might also happen that an enormous whale came swimming by. Then it would get dark everywhere the whale broke through the seaweed as when a cloud moves in front of the sun. And when it made a crashing slam with its strong tail, the seaweed shook as though an earthquake were occurring.

One time, when a ship sailed over the seaweed stand, a seaman fell overboard and was swallowed promptly by a large shark which consumed him in a single mouthful and swam on with a full stomach and a clear conscience.

It was easy to appreciate that it was lovely to be in a seaweed stand, but mostly it was quiet and still because there were no animals singing or shouting.

In the middle of the seaweed stand, there happened to be a cozy open place between the crowns of the branches, and near to the ocean's surface. The water was warm and clear, situated so that only rarely did anyone venture inside. It was here that four youngsters played every day with each other, and chatted about what little ones talk about.

All four of them were so tiny you couldn't see them with the naked eye. If someone had come with a magnifying glass and discovered them, he still would have had difficulty seeing who was who unless he knew an awful lot about nature.

That was because they were all round, transparent, and with fine hairs, but lacking heads and legs and eyes and everything you expect to find in a common animal—and humans too, can't manage well without them!

They had nothing common among them.. One of them was the offspring of a star coral, the second of a jellyfish, and the third of a starfish. But the fourth one was a genuine young oyster.

One day they were chatting about what they wanted to be when they grew up.

"I'd like to be a predator!" said the little starfish. "I'll hide in the seaweed stand, and jump out at the mussels, small fish, and all the animals I can overpower, and suck out the last drop of blood in them."

"I will swim around and just look beautiful," said the jellyfish. "And if anyone gets too close, I'll just use my stinger."

"I'm made for something better," pouted the oyster youngster, looking as important as it could since it had neither face nor eyes.

"Really?" questioned the starfish. "Where did you learn that?"

"You are just born with it," replied the little oyster haughtily. "You know, to humans I'm a domesticated animal. It is unbelievable how much they appreciate me; they idolize me. Some of them do nothing but breed me, take care of me, and then sell me so others can consume me. They build lovely, large water shelters for me with sticks I can cling to firmly."

"Actually, I think it's you that is seeking all the attention you can get from people," said the little jellyfish. "But each to his own. I can't think of anything more awful than clinging to a stick."

"Please, just allow me a quiet, undisturbed life until I am eaten," said the little oyster.

During all this chatter, the coral youngster didn't say a word, but bobbed its hair-like appendages in the water, listening to the others. And no one thought anything of it because the star coral was always the most laid back of them all, and so they didn't think it mattered. But finally the starfish asked a question:

"Well, coral, what about you? What are you going to do? Have you thought about it?"

"I think of nothing else but the future," replied the coral youngster.

"Well now," said the starfish. "Will you tell us what you're hoping for?"

"You wouldn't be able to comprehend it even if I told you," said the coral.

"Just try anyway," argued the starfish.

And the oyster youngster and little jellyfish agreed.

"When I grow up, I will build myself an island," said the little coral.

"What... ?" erupted the other three simultaneously.

"An island," repeated the coral.

"You're not going cheap," said the starfish laughing so much its whole body shook. "How are you going to manage that?"

"I don't know yet," answered the coral, "but an island I will build... a decent island which rises from the water, and has a good hold when the waves crash against it."

"It's amazing that you care about that," said the oyster.

"It gives me the shivers just to hear about anything so permanent," said the jellyfish.

So all three of them teased the coral, which didn't mind at all, but continued to bob with its hairy appendages in the water whispering to itself.

"It has to be a decent island, one with palm trees and birds. Starfish and jellyfish will swim around in the water, and the waves will wash them ashore where they will lie and rot in the sun. The island will have people who eat the oysters."

When the others got bored with teasing the coral they all became good friends again, swimming around in a little area of the seaweed growth, eating animals even smaller than themselves. They were happy as young and satisfied sea-life with their routines.

Chapter 2

Sometime later, still in the seaweed stand, the four youngsters had all grown up. The oyster youngster had gotten its shell, and it sat on a rock at the bottom of the ocean yawning, letting the salt water flow into it. The body of starfish had sprung out five pointed arms which reached out into the water on all sides, and the animal resembled the star that sits on top of a Christmas tree.

Twice a fish had bitten off one arm, which was of no concern to the starfish, because a new arm grew out again promptly; then the starfish was as good as new, able to crawl around in the seaweed stand as a prominent predator, something it had dreamed about since its earliest days.

The jellyfish wasn't so lucky. One day while in the company of other recently grown up jellyfish, conversing somewhere in the seaweed stand, a whale came swimming by with its wide mouth open and ate them. There were thousands of jellyfish and they all disappeared together, swept into the whale's stomach.

But now, the fully developed coral youngster moved from the safe, comfortable place of its earliest days, and allowed the waves to carry it far away from the seaweed stand.

The coral searched around for a long time to find a place it would like to live in, and, at last, it found one, way around on the other side of the submerged mountain. No seaweed grew there, where the water was clean, clear, salty, and wonderfully warm, and just there it settled down.

It developed arms just like the starfish, but a lot more of them, and these arms positioned themselves like a wreath around its mouth, for now it had both a mouth and a stomach. After a while, it noticed that it had become hardened and anchored both below and inside itself, and before realizing it, there was a respectable amount of calcium inside it too.

"Now it's coming!" it thought, very pleased with itself. "It's the beginning of the island."

One day a bud shot out from one side—just like from trees on land—and the bud became the loveliest star coral with arms and mouth and stomach, and a calcified material inside it. But it sat there anchored to the old coral just like a branch stays on a tree. The first coral was exceedingly pleased.

"That will help!" it said. "Now we are two."

The first coral described the island it wanted to construct, and the new coral was in agreement about how it should look. And so they both broke out with new buds until fairly soon they had created a lovely coral colony with many branches all full of star corals. The whole day they swayed with their arms in the water, scooping up tiny animals into their hungry mouths.

One day the starfish came by, appearing amazed, and it never recognized its old playmate.

"You're quite an odd tree with flowers out!" it said.

"I am not some tree," said the first coral. "I am a star coral."

"Heavens! Is it you?" said the starfish. "It's surprising how much you've changed. Really, I wouldn't have know you anymore."

"Likewise," said the coral. "But we haven't seen each other since we were youngsters. Now I'm building my island."

"Are you still thinking of that ridiculous project?" asked the starfish laughing. "I thought you had gotten wiser with age. So, you think you've become an entire enterprise?"

“That’s right,” agreed the coral, “I grew branches and budded out from them, so all the flowers you see are coral polyps that are in the same enterprise with me all around the island.”

“I see,” said the starfish. “That’s clever of you because by yourself you wouldn’t have gotten anywhere. Are you all getting on together?”

“Splendidly!” replied the coral. You couldn’t find a better, more solid, family relationship. We stick together through thick and thin. Just think of it this way: When one of us eats well, we all find pleasure in that.”

“That seems to take your enterprise idea too far,” said the starfish. When I find a tasty morsel to eat, I don’t want it going into someone else’s stomach.”

"You don't understand me," said the coral, but the starfish wasn't interested.

"Bye, bye!" said the starfish. "And good luck with the island."

When its old friend had gone, the first coral, sitting at the bottom of the enlarging colony, whispered to the bud closest to it.

"You are me, and I am you, and they can never separate us. We belong together, and we will do the same thing—we will build the island."

The bud repeated this to the next bud, and so on until there wasn't a single coral in the whole colony that didn't get the message. As it accumulated more and more branches, the corals had more and more newborns that swam out into the water—small, tiny, transparent nothings with fine hairs on them. They enjoyed their freedom as youngsters, but they had the island on their minds constantly. As they matured, they pushed out buds and attached themselves firmly to the side of the colony.

"I can't do it anymore," said the first coral one day, but it had plenty of help.

All around that old coral, an entire forest of star corals was growing up. Their white branches were all entangled with each other, and from them shone the loveliest star blossoms. They shot out new buds constantly, which sent out millions of tiny coral offspring. And as they continued to build and build without end, the island was always on their minds.

The old coral could be proud of its work, for it was now the great-great-great-great grandparent of the whole coral colony

"Don't forget the island!" said the first coral, and then it died. The water washed the dead body away, but where it had been, the remains of it shone like a star on the coral branch.

Chapter 3

Many, many, many years passed, but it made not the slightest difference for the ocean waves rolled in without stop as they always did, the sun still shone and the storms raged. The now torn-up seaweed where the coral youngsters once played had washed away, but other plants had grown up in their place, and new seaweed stands developed on the underwater mountain.

The sea turtles which grazed there had died many years ago, but new sea turtles replaced them. Gone were the oysters, the starfish, and the multi-colored fish that swam amidst the coral branches. Even the enormous whale that ate all the jellyfish in one mouthful took a harpoon in the neck and got cut up and boiled down for its oil.

But even though the old ones were all gone, the next generation took over, looking just like those who came before them and acting like they did, so it wasn't possible to see any real changes in life where the old seaweed stand had been. But on the other side, where the original coral youngster had attached itself to build an island, things looked very different.

An enormous number of coral branches had developed, and still more were coming. Millions of tiny coral offspring swam out into the world, came home and attached themselves next to their parents. Millions of the animals died. In many of the branches, not a single living coral remained, but all the hard calcified remains were full of reminders, looking like stars where once they had attached themselves.

The waves had overturned the old, dead coral branches, breaking them up into stumps and pieces, throwing them in between and on top of one another. Eventually, it transformed into a large and imposing limestone rock that was continuously enlarging because the new offspring attached themselves firmly on top of the old coral colony. They continued to build with great industry until, one day, they had finally reached close to the surface.

"Now we'll have an island!" they said to each other happily. "If only our great-great-great-great-grandparent had lived to see it now!"

But they had celebrated too early, for when they were ready to rise above the water, they couldn't. The youngest corals could not tolerate the sun shining on them, and despite how hard they tried, they could not make any headway.

"It's time to help you," said the waves, and they lifted a couple of large coral masses up from the ocean's bottom, and flung them on top of the others.

The island was lying there now. It wasn't large, but it was white and shone beautifully in the sun. All around it, as far as you could see, there was nothing but water, water, and more water.

One day, a large white seagull came flying in and landed on the island, and the earth, trying to simply spin around the sun as usual, was in quite a bad mood. The moon was teasing it mercilessly, and it was more disgruntled when it discovered a bulge it had not seen before.

"Now what the devil is that?" the earth moaned.

It was only the coral island, but when the earth learned what had been going on, it became angry.

"Things have gone far enough now!" it yelled out. "Not only am I made a fool of by an arrogant comet, I have to put up with being smirked at by an impoverished moon every month. Not only are people rummaging around in my innards, converting land to water and water to land, now I have to put up with tiny coral nothings ganging up with each other and building an island right in my midsection. Enough is enough and there'll be no more!

"Suddenly, the whole ocean bottom caved in right where the coral island lay, and that was very frightening! The coral island

disappeared into the ocean, and the seagull that was sitting on it flew away screaming. The massive blocks of coral tumbled down on each other, breaking into bits and pieces.

Fish, crayfish and sea turtles fled as fast as they could, and every leaf in the seaweed stand was trembling.

When, once again there was calm in the ocean, the corals whispered to each other:

"Remember the island!"

They regrouped, gathered up their strength, and started building again until eventually they had reached the surface of the ocean, helped by the waves that hurled enormous rocks up from the bottom, and the island arose again.

"Well, can you believe it!" said the earth, and caused the bottom of the ocean to collapse again, making it even deeper.

"Remember the island!" said the corals and a long while later, the island reappeared.

"Can you all be so stubborn?" said the earth.

"Indeed, we can," said the corals.

"All right then, I give up," said the earth: "I can't go on like this."

Chapter 4

The island was now permanently secured, deep down, to the side of the mountain. The corals continued to build without stopping, and the waves hurled up more and more rocks, and the island became bigger and bigger. Then, one day, a large, round, brown object came sailing in and slammed against one side of the island.

"Who's there?" inquired the corals down in the water.

"It's me!" said the object.

"What? Who is 'me'?" asked the corals again.

"Don't you know me?" said the object. "I'm a coconut, renowned over the entire world. I'm the one that converts islands into spots on the map which get into geography books. I've even had little verses made up about me. One of them begins like this..."

"A coconut floated on the ocean waves..."

"That may be so," interrupted the corals, "but that doesn't interest us. We have built this island ourselves and have never had time to recite silly poems."

"Well, it's amazing how much ignorance exists in the world," said the coconut. "Hmm... do you have enough soil so I can send down roots and grow up into a palm tree?"

"Aha!" whispered the corals to each other. "It's a palm tree!"

Now things were very different, and they then politely asked the coconut to return after a while which would give them time to make soil for it to grow in the best way they knew how.

"Great!" said the coconut. "I can just bob around on the ocean for a year seeing as how thick my shell is. I can stand it."

So the coconut floated away, and every time there was loose seaweed, or a dead fish or starfish, or almost anything in the water, the corals asked the waves if they would please fling it up onto the island. The waves obliged, and these things rotted, turning into soil. The marine birds came too, and from their droppings, a cherry pit fell on the ground, took root, and grew up into a lovely little tree.

One day a large, hollow log came floating in and, after landing on the island, it rotted, dispersing a lot of grass seeds. Soon, the whole island was green. There were also two lizards and some newborns in the log, and they decided that the island was quite a nice place to settle.

And then the coconut came back.

"Lift me up to shore!" it said to the waves, and so they did, and the coconut settled down to grow.

It sprouted and became a magnificent tree. Its coconuts fell all around, and soon a whole grove of coconut trees had appeared on the island. Birds came, built nests in the trees, then flowers, bees, more birds, and butterflies arrived.

One day, a rather desperate man sailed in on a life raft. His ship had gone down, and he had weathered the sea for many days. He was both hungry and thirsty, and when he saw the island, he was wild with joy. He clambered onto the land, ate coconuts and oysters, and built a make-shift house to live in until a ship could come to return him to his homeland.

But down in the water, the coral continued to work away without stopping, for they could never make the island big enough.

"Oh, if only our great-great-great-great-great-great-great-great great grandparent could see it!" they said to each other.

Natural Enemies

Chapter 1

The spruce forest towered mightily over all the other forests. It spread up and down the slopes, dominating the landscape. As the wind blew across the hills and dales, the spruces whistled softly knowing their undisputed power.

"God bless my spruce forest," said the forester. "It takes care of itself with no troublesome hitches and it puts money in the till. I'd be perfectly happy if I only had spruces in the forest."

"We are masters of the forest," said the spruces.

"But it's ugly in there, spruces," said the hedge nearly drowning in flowers that surrounded the forest "Look how bright I am and note my fragrance! There's not a flower on you!"

"But flowers just wither and die!" replied the spruces. "You're bragging now, but in a month, you'll be empty and ugly. My needles may turn brown but new green ones always come straightaway, and in the fall, I have my wondrous mushrooms in red, white, and yellow, so poisonous and strange that you're even afraid of them in the dark. And then I have my moss, delicate, peaceful and green."

"It's so rigid in there, spruces," said the beeches. You're all straight up and down, one tree the same as the other—'one-two, one-two'—like soldiers in formation. You provide no shade, and where are your murmuring brooks? Where are your birds?"

"And where are you in winter?" replied the spruces. "Look at us. We'll stay green right through winter. We're always the same, unchanging with no screaming, with no crying, even as our leaves renew themselves. We stand tall, quiet, and dignified."

"It's so boring in there, spruces," said the meadow. "Not a bee buzzes around, not a bright butterfly anywhere."

"Are we supposed to believe you are actually happy with your animal visitors?" said the spruces. "They eat your roots, they eat your leaves, they eat your berries. We're satisfied with our fine, hard-working ants."

Chapter 2

One day, a butterfly entered the spruce forest. It was white with black splotches and looked so modest and innocent it captivated the biggest old spruce on whose branch it alighted.

"Such a lovely little lady," said the spruce. "May I ask your name?"

"I am known as the nun," said the butterfly with a sweet little voice. "I would like your permission to lay a few eggs on your stems."

"Oh, by all means," said the old spruce. "With great pleasure. As many as you want. There is plenty of space as you can see."

"There'll probably be a few more butterflies coming along," said the nun softly and modestly. "We're just a small family."

"Oh, sure," said the old spruce, "make yourselves at home."

But a 'few more' was not quite right, and about fifty nun butterflies settled on the old spruce and even more on some other spruces standing nearby. In the afternoon, another swarm arrived, and the next day still more, and they kept coming.

The spruces chatted to each other about this and were enormously proud of the pleasant sights in the housing they were providing. If there were a spruce tree with no butterflies on it, the others looked upon it with pity or scorn. All the nuns were modest and grateful.

"You are much too kind to us," they said to the spruces.

"We rarely get such distinguished visitors," said the spruces sighing with their long branches.

But the nuns didn't say much and did nothing else but lay their eggs.

"I suppose that larvae will come out of the eggs?" inquired the old spruce.

"Likely," said the nun that had arrived there first.

"Just look at all of us!" the spruces said proudly to the meadow, the beeches, and the hedges. "Do you see our lovely butterflies? They're not a bunch of braggarts like you've got; they're quiet, reserved females. They are laying their eggs on our branches, and soon some larvae will appear."

"Well, good luck with that" said the beeches; the meadow and the hedges agreed.

After a while, all the nuns died. They fell to the ground with a modest sigh, and the spruces sprinkled their fragrant needles on them and hummed a choral piece over them.

Then the larvae appeared, and the trees had plenty to do just watching them.

They were nothing like their mothers and weren't pretty at all. They were about an inch long with a gray-green color just like the spruces' trunks. They had stiff brushes on both sides of their bodies, a large head with a couple of sharp mouth-parts, and two awful, greedy-looking eyes, reminding you of hungry pigs.

"What do you want then, you youngsters?" asked the spruces.

"Food!" screamed the larvae all together. They crawled up the trunk, out along the branches, and began consuming the spruces' juicy green needles.

"That's quite a respectable appetite," said the spruces, nodding to each other. "But, let's not worry ourselves over a few lost needles."

But it was somewhat more than a couple of needles that disappeared, and toward the end of summer, the old spruce that had accepted the first nuns was on the verge of giving up. Miserable, if it could do math, it could have easily counted the number of green needles remaining, and the other neighboring spruces didn't appear to be much better off.

"That was really quite an effort," said the old spruce. "I don't believe at my age I'd do it again."

"Nor me... nor me... nor me...," sighed all the other spruces.

All the larvae had now pupated, with lovely, small brown cocoons that glistened like bronze and gold when the sun shone.

"It's lovely again now," said the old spruce, but its voice was weak, and there was no ring in it.

"How's it going with your beautiful butterflies?" teased the meadow.

"You don't seem to be so green this autumn as you usually are!" mocked the beeches.

"I think you're just as plain and ugly as I am," said the hedge.

The spruces said nothing so as not to appear to be complaining, but the others were entirely right.

Winter came with its snow and its storms. More branches fell down than usual, and one night the old spruce toppled to the ground with a resounding crash.

"I wouldn't have thought that could happen to this tree," said the forester the next morning as he prepared to chop up the old spruce. "I would have expected it to live for many more years."

"It's the nuns...." whispered the old spruce just before it died.

Chapter 3

Spring came, and the spruces put out new buds thinking they should make up for lost time. All the twigs had small, light green bud-scales, and a good mood prevailed as the spruces still considered themselves to be the masters of the forest.

But on the first warm summer's day, all the pupae cases burst as if on command, and out flew the lovely nuns by the thousands. They appeared so modest and innocent, just like their parents, but there were so many that the spruces shivered right down to their roots.

"Oh, no! oh, no!" they begged. "We can't take this anymore. You must go somewhere else."

"We only want to lay a few eggs on your trunk," said the nuns softly and modestly.

And while the spruces protested, and stretched their half-naked stems towards the sky, the nuns settled on the trunks and laid their eggs. Afterwards they fell down and died, like their mothers had done, but this time no spruce needles were sprinkled on them, and no choral music was hummed, for there was no sorrow left at all; indeed, there were hardly any needles or humming voices left.

When the time came, the larvae appeared, and there were so many they couldn't be counted at all.

"Food!" they all screamed.

"We have no food," said the spruces dejectedly.

But the larvae went to town on the remaining young shoots and gorged themselves until they were sleek and fat.

When they finished with one branch, they made a long stretch and lowered themselves down to another branch. When they dropped to the ground, they crawled up the next trunk, and the whole spruce forest was in despair.

"Our number is up," sighed the spruces.

"Food!" shouted the larvae.

"There are some brutal creatures in my wonderful forest," said the forester. "What can I possibly do?"

When fall came, the larvae pupated, and as winter arrived, trees toppled over as never before. By summer, there was such a terrible mess, and half of the spruces in the forest had died. There were now so many nuns, the spruces appeared to be covered with snow in the wrong season.

When the wind came, it blew many of the butterflies into the lake covering the water with an inch-thick layer of stuck-together wings. But still so many larvae were born that the spruces' branches touched the ground under their weight. The larvae all swarmed together, stepping on each other, and the trees looked like a mass of living vermin.

The spruces said nothing. They had long ago given up protesting, and the remaining ones waited silently and quietly for death to come. Every hour in the day, one of them toppled, and branches and tree trunks blocked all the roads that ran through the forest.

The old forester could barely get around and sat quietly on a fallen trunk, wringing his hands as tears ran down his cheeks. "My forest, my beautiful forest," he said. "It is not in man's power to save you."

But even as he was saying this, something he could not see because he was getting old, was getting to work, becoming busier and busier in the spruce's part of the forest.

It looked like small black dots, which hovered in massive swarms in the air around the trees, but it was actually nimble female parasitic wasps sticking their egg depositors into fat nun larvae and leaving an egg mass behind.

Out of these eggs hatched wasp larvae, and as the young of the nuns were eating the spruce branches, the young of the wasps were feeding on the living bodies of those fat and greedy nun larvae.

At the end of the summer, there were scarcely any nun pupae left. The dried, cracked casings of the nuns' larvae bodies were all over the twigs, and inside them the parasitic wasps pupated snugly through the winter.

Chapter 4

In the following spring, there were only a few nuns, but an enormous number of parasitic wasps.

The forester strolled through the woods alongside a man with a box on his back for collecting plant specimens. This man was a field biologist, who understood plants and animals, insects especially, better than most people, and he had ventured out to observe the abominable destruction of the spruce forest.

The forester told him how mighty and magnificent all the spruce trees had been in the old days and pointed out to him where so many of the trees had fallen. Now, the scattered, crisscrossed trunks and boughs were dead, with raspberries and ferns growing up between them. It was as quiet as a human graveyard, as the sun bore down on the last remains of the once magnificent spruces.

"It's all over now," said the forester, "but they also destroyed most of the forest. Last year, it looked like snow everywhere for all the nuns that were here. This year there are hardly any. I don't understand how this could have happened."

"The parasitic wasps made it happen," said the biologist, and he then explained to the forester what had taken place.

"Then God bless the parasitic wasps," said the forester. "They are the most marvelous creatures in creation."

"They're no better than the nuns," said the field biologist.

"You are joking... right?" replied the forester.

"I'm certainly not," said the biologist, "and the spruces are not better than the nuns, either. They all deserve to live... and why not?"

"Now that's the limit," said the forester angrily. "What was the point of all that destruction?"

The scientist looked away into the downfallen forest, quietly put the plant specimen box he was carrying on the ground and sat down on a fallen bough.

"Let me tell you something," he said. "There were too many spruces here and, as nature requires, the nuns came to destroy them. Then there were too many nuns, so the parasitic wasps came to destroy them. This is what we might call the policing of nature, or maybe just nature's way of maintaining the right balance among its creatures. The two insects are natural enemies, you see. In nature, every living creature connects with others in ways that work for the benefit of the whole. Doesn't that make sense?"

"If you look up," continued the field biologist, "you will see what an enormous number of parasitic wasps there are. They will die without getting their eggs laid because they have nothing to lay them in. Believe me, they wish that the forest was full of nun pupae for them to use again."

"And I wish it was full of spruces again," said the forester.

"It may not be in your time, but you can count on them coming back," said the scientist, "as you can that the nuns will return, and then the parasitic wasps once more. As long as the earth revolves, so will nature's cycles continue. Without that, we'd all be just spruce trees."

The Wily Fox

Chapter 1

It was a sultry night in July, the kind people say they really look forward to during the long winter. They still protest the lack of warm days when they do not come in the summer but then, when they do arrive and even though there aren't very many of them, they insist they can't stand it.

It was the season of the light nights in Denmark, and you could see everything almost as in the daytime. There were many who couldn't sleep because it was too warm, but they weathered it in very different ways. Some cursed and hollered, threw off their covers, and were disagreeable and uncomfortable. They were the old folks. After they had laid down a while, others got out of bed, looked through the window into the light night, put on a few clothes, and walked out into the green woods or down onto the beach where the waves sang softly, yet forcefully, even though it was still. This was the young ones.

The animals naturally accepted it, but not according to age or mood. It was as though nature decided it herself, and there was no point grumbling. While those who had been working during the day were sleeping safely through the night, others had been sleeping the whole day long in their holes and hideaways, only to awaken at sunset. Now they ventured out with keen eyes and an empty stomach to get their share of life's pleasures.

One such creature was the owl, mocked and badly treated by the other birds if he showed himself in the sunshine. Only at night could he really see. When it was dark for others, he could see everything with great clarity. Silently, he flew among the branches in order not to alert his prey. With lightning speed, he'd swoop down on it, either eating it at once, or taking it up with him to the old hollow oak tree. Here he had his nest, and he would give his catch to his starving youngsters, who waited with open mouths and bulging eyes; they too were already becoming accustomed to being alert at night when an owl's work begins.

The owl's favorite prey, the wood mouse, was also out at night. It didn't like to venture out during the day, as tiny, soft and helpless as it was, unable to defend itself against crows, buzzards, and others who would eat it if they could. Another who made the night his own was the fox who wanted no one to see his route to the farmer's henhouse. He could also snack on a small, delicious mouse with great pleasure because he never knew if he'd dine on chicken that night. Tonight, the fox also wondered if the farmer had fixed his fence after his last two ducklings got snatched from under his nose.

The moth too, that night brooding over her short and difficult life, flew out after the sun had gone down because she didn't care to deal with all the elaborate flowers that attracted the butterflies the whole day long. She only wanted a little nectar before laying her eggs and dying.

She scarcely needed all those bright colors her daytime competitors had. They shimmered in such a way you couldn't really tell the difference between them and the flowers they fluttered in and out of. If the moth had resembled the flowers she went to, a hungry bat would quickly have snatched her on its own night hunt.

The moth's favorite camouflage was a gray-brown coat, which almost never revealed where she was. She also knew where to find the nectar in a plain, unassuming flower that also kept itself hidden when the sun was out. This was the rocket flower that, somewhat like the moth, preferred not to compete with the fancy flowers in the meadow, which in their entire splendor, tempted all the other daytime insects to visit. There were just too many competing then, so it was much better to take on a plain appearance.

Therefore, the rocket flower resting by the bushes stood warm and radiant in the daytime, but when darkness came to the forest, it sent out the most fragrant and inviting aroma as if speaking to the moth. And when the moth got a whiff of that aroma, she easily traced her way to her modest friend, alighting on its petals.

"I'm here, little rocket flower! Now give me your nectar and let me load your sticky pollen grains onto my roughened wings, and I promise you I'll carry them over to another rocket flower."

There were many others also out in this wonderfully warm July night, but let's talk about the nightingale because she was not exactly quiet. She had nothing at all to do in the nighttime because she was a day bird that had done her work and cared for her family all before the sun went down. But it appeared as though she was precisely like those restless young people who also couldn't sleep on such a lovely warm night.

Outside her nest in the big lilac bush, she sang as though her little throat was about to burst. She sang about how beautiful the night was, of life's happiness, and she sang and sang, and kept on singing for her own pleasure, without caring whether anyone was listening to her. She knew summers were short, lasting only two months in Denmark, by which time her young ones would have grown up, ready to fly south where it was warm, and the air was full of flies and other tasty things.

But that night, it thrilled her to sit and sing in the forest ranger's garden, where she had built her nest three years in a row, and she surely hoped to return to for years to come.

Chapter 2

Nearby, the fox was returning from his excursions and had found a new fence around the farmer's henhouse which, for sure, was so tight no one could break through it. He had not encountered even the tiniest mouse on his trip, and he was feeling especially hungry.

Before he slipped out of the garden again and back into the forest, he stood quietly for a moment, listening under the lilac bush where the nightingale was singing. She spied him and stopped singing momentarily as she hopped up to the highest branch. Here she hit a couple of cheery notes and looked with scorn down at the fox.

"It didn't go so well for you, red fox," she said.

"Oh, you've heard about it already?" said the fox sitting on his tail. "It must have been the doves that told you. They flew up as I shook the fence looking for a way in, and they sure are a bunch of terrible gossipers."

"What are you talking about?" asked the nightingale. "I haven't seen or heard any doves, and I don't understand a word you're saying."

"I'm talking about my midnight trip to the farmer's henhouse," replied the fox. "What else would I be talking about? Wasn't that what you meant when you said it wasn't going so well? Or are you thinking about the mouse that got away from me over at the beech tree?"

"I'm not talking about any of them at all," explained the nightingale. "It's just that you have so many dirty tricks up your sleeve that no one can keep track. I was referring to the fact that I was sitting too low, and you could have easily snapped me up, but I saw you in time and hopped up to the top of the bush. I know you, red fox, and I know what to expect of your crooked nature. You were the one that ate my grandmother."

"Was I?" asked the fox casually, lying down with his head on his paws. "Then your grandmother must have been very careless, or otherwise, I wouldn't have been able to get her. If I were a bird, no fox would ever catch me."

"Not likely," said the nightingale. "And if you had wings, you'd soon catch me, wouldn't you?"

"Sure," said the fox. "I'm hungry, and I'd eat you even if you didn't taste so good. Why shouldn't I? Don't you eat when you're hungry? Everyone has to eat to survive."

"Yes, of course," answered the nightingale. "But I eat flies and gnats and other vermin designed for munching, but to eat a sweet, innocent songbird? Never!"

"Oh no," said the fox yawning. "I kind of agree with you; I doubt if you'd eat the old goose, the forest ranger's duck, or the buck that forages down in the meadow. Each takes only what he can get his teeth into."

"You're always trying to talk your way out of things," said the nightingale. "But, believe me, I saw you settle under the bush with your disgusting grin, trying to look like my song delighted you. You're too well known in the forest, red fox. You won't fool anyone again, except for the biggest jackasses who deserve nothing better."

"Then I heartily wish that a fat jackass would come along that I could make a fool of because I'm starving," said the fox. "But you've got it all wrong. I really think you sing nicely, and I stopped here just to listen to you. When my stomach is empty, I'm in the best mood for chatting and listening to music because it takes my mind off my hunger."

"What do you prefer doing when your stomach is full?" asked the nightingale. "Would it be better to sing to you with the last bit of goose thigh hanging out of your mouth?"

"Not really," replied the fox. "When I'm satisfied, I only want to sleep and dream about getting more food. I know nothing more satisfying after a good hunt than to lope home and lie down in my den and sleep the whole day away, dreaming of ducks, chickens, and geese or some other poetic creatures. Then I wake up in the evening happy, contented, fresh, and ready to go again.

"But regarding the situation now, the thought of catching you today had never even crossed my mind. Of course, if you had just

flopped down into my mouth, I would have eaten you— the little of you there is—because it would just have been so easy."

The nightingale shuddered at the thought as the fox lay on his side with all four legs outstretched and with his eyes half-closed.

"Despicable behavior," muttered the nightingale as her blood ran cold.

"But the thing is," continued the fox, "I remember your grandmother now and she had no taste at all. No, it's true; I'm not really that keen on nightingales, so can you now relax enough to sing some more for me?"

"You're a horrible villain, the worst," said the nightingale, deeply offended. "Devouring a sweet old lady. Aren't you the least bit ashamed to tell me that story? What a cruel, sly and evil creature you are, you won't get another note out of me. Do you think I'd sing for a scoundrel like you, the worst monster in the entire forest? If you were down and out, and begged me on bended knees, you wouldn't get a tune out of me."

"Now wait a second, my dear nightingale," argued the fox. "Do you really think a well-traveled duchess like you should come out with that old nonsense about me and my sly character? It's enough that everyone else in the forest amuses themselves with that kind of nonsense without you joining in. What will be will be, and I won't comment about that. Most of the name-callers and do-gooders haven't been out in the world; most of them haven't even been outside the perimeters of this forest. But you, who has traveled and seen so much, is that all you care about?"

"You talk as though you're different and better than everyone else in the forest," sneered the nightingale.

"But I am," said the fox in quite a matter-of-fact way. "First, I wasn't born here in the forest but came into this world way over on the other side of the country, north from here, past two watering holes."

"Then how in the world did you get over here?" asked the nightingale. "Can you swim, or did you possibly have wings once and lose them on one of your vile outings?"

"Well now, there you go again with being horrible when I've only just met you," he sighed. "As we already talked about, why do you care at all? No, I've never had wings, and if I did, I'd still have them. Naturally, I can swim well but don't do so except under the most extreme circumstances. As for getting here, I didn't expect that because I arrived here courtesy of the government."

"What's that?" asked the nightingale, astounded. "Do you now want me to believe the humans had gone to any expense for a fellow like you?"

"I will not kid you about anything," replied the fox with a sigh. "It is exactly like I'm telling you. I came here courtesy of the government. I was one of 21 fox kittens—and a cute bunch we were too—and I wasn't the worst of the lot!"

"We had just finished suckling on mom when they yanked us from her and put us in a box. That's where I met my first mate, incidentally; she was a real sweetie. As soon as we got here and fixed up a decent space in the ground, we started living together. Altogether, we had 19 little ones, and two of them are now living at the other end of the forest. They're doing fine, I imagine, but hunters beating the underbrush shot fifteen of their siblings including their mother."

"I see," said the nightingale, struggling to feel sorry for the fox. Could she believe his story?

"Are you telling me they shot your mate and your fifteen youngsters, and now you want me to believe they transported you over two watering holes, plus many miles, all at the expense of the government?"

"Whether or not you believe me, is your business, as I already said. The fact is that the government is a strange organization, and they can barely get things to work. Sometimes, they have too many foxes, and then they have too few. Over here they've shot and killed nearly all the foxes with their rotten hunting outings and those damn beaters. That's what I call a dirty trick. You can characterize them with all those words you labeled me with before. They are the monsters, the bandits, and the evil ones."

"Unfortunately, I don't agree with you again," replied the nightingale. "I'm on the best of possible terms with those humans who adore me and my songs and protect me in every way."

"Oh, do they?" sneered the fox. "I'm sure they have many ridiculous ideas. However, this idea of us sticking together is something you shouldn't worry yourself over. You'll see, we'll become best friends, and no one will separate us."

"That would be weird," said the nightingale. "But tell me more about how you got here. I find it hard to believe, but it still interests me."

"That's better," said the fox. "Well now, where were we? Oh yes, the government. First, they shot so many of us, but then came to regret that enormously because, after a while, they couldn't believe the number of mice that appeared. These mice ate the roots of the grass and young trees, and swarmed everywhere, so the humans soon realized the mice would devour everything in the forest. Now the authorities worried about not having any foxes, and so they trapped us, sent us over here, releasing us into the forest to deal with the mice."

"Oh really," was all the nightingale could think to say. She had never heard of humans wanting foxes before. No other creature, either.

"We then feasted freely on the mice, but after a while, those stupid humans forgot how they had needed us before and shot wildly at us again. It's also possible they thought we sacrificed too many chickens and some other vermin, but we need variation sometimes because a fox can't live on mice alone. Regardless, they continued the massacres, and they killed a lot of us. And if they continue—as they probably will—they soon must import some new foxes, the dopes that they are."

"Well, you're entitled to your opinion," said the nightingale. "Humans are the smartest of all the animals; they have songs, and music, and everything."

"They also understand the feel of a fox skin," said the fox with a shudder. "They hunt me down for my fur as well as to save their precious chickens."

The nightingale did not reply to this, but the fox did not seem too worried that its death might be imminent. He stretched luxuriously, and then he quietly rubbed himself on the branches of the lilac bush until it started shaking.

"Are you trying to shake me down?" asked the nightingale. "You can spare yourself the trouble. I'm sitting here more securely than ever."

"You're starting up again with your ridiculous ideas," sighed the fox. "I've told you already, but please allow me to repeat myself: I'm not expecting anything from you, other than you sing me one of your delightful songs. Aren't you embarrassed to say things like that? I'm sure you've been around in the world, and I suppose you've seen the lions in Africa, eagles in the sky, and many strange sights. I'm sure you can eat a fly with the same enjoyment I get from a chicken, and you'd readily tear apart a pretty butterfly for your youngsters in the same way I would rip a white goose apart for mine. It's tit for tat for both of us, so why all this nonsense? Leave that for the barnyard animals and let us talk like adults as long as we agree not to eat each other. This arguing is boring, so please spare me. If you really have nothing else to say, I'd rather that you went back to your singing."

Chapter 3

Now the nightingale, quite flattered by the fox's words, decided she wouldn't let on, and remained suspicous. "So why are you shaking the branches so much? I'm sure you really want me to fall down."

"But why would I want to do that?" asked the fox frustratedly. "Actually, I'm rubbing myself because of all these damn fleas who've taken a home in my fur. But you know nothing about that horrible annoyance, I suppose?"

"Oh, but I do!" replied the nightingale, hopping further down the bush out of sheer curiosity, wondering if the fox had the same fleas. “I don’t know of any worse torment than being bitten all the time by fleas.”

“Neither do I,” said the fox, having another welcome scratch on the bush. “To be honest with you, they give me more grief than anything else in the world. There are so damn many of them in my fur, and they are so persistent. An ordinary animal rests between meals, but fleas just keep biting away both day and night. I’d be willing to put up with one more fox hunter’s chase a year if I could always be free of these fleas.”

“Yes, I agree with you,” said the nightingale. “They are a horrible plague.”

“Really? Now I thought birds were immune to fleas,” said the fox, seeming quite surprised.

“Oh my, how could you believe that? No one is more bothered by all kinds of vermin than we birds are. Some of us can’t handle them at all. I had an aunt whose own lice and fleas were eating her alive.”

“Oh dear, but that’s horrible,” said the fox, “but what about the fleas; what’s your solution?”

“Well, I roll around in some dry dirt, or dusty soil, or sand out on the road,” said the nightingale. “I puff out my feathers and fill my body up with bits of dust or sand. Then I stand up again, and shake the bits out, which takes out some of those pesky vermin.”

“It sounds clever of you,” said the fox. “I think I’ll try that myself some time. Can you show me how it’s done? Here’s a lovely dry patch of earth just large enough for you to shake yourself in. Come on down here and try it.”

“Well, thanks a lot,” came the response. “It looks perfect, just as I like it, but I never take a bath when there is a fox around watcing me.”

“Of course,” said the fox. “I forgot. You have your modesty to think about. Dare I ask at what time of the day you take your bath?

You understand, I'm only asking in order not to embarrass you by mistake."

"Many thanks for your concern," said the nightingale. "I have only one definite bathing time, and that's when a fox is not present."

* * *

The dawn was rising in the east, and the birds were awakening in their nests, peeping out a little, as the nightingale hummed to herself. The fox seemed to be relaxing with his eyes shut, but he was really watching the nightingale the whole time. Then the nightingale shook herself again and, recalling the fox's problem with fleas, decided her's were biting even more.

"Tell me, red fox," she said, "what do you do with your fleas?"

"Oh, well now, to tell you the truth, I rarely do anything except have a scratch on a tree. But when they are a real nuisance, I use the water cure."

"The water cure?" said the nightingale. "What's that?"

"I really would like to show it to you," said the fox, "even though you won't show me your method. There's a little water hole outside the garden gate. It's just deep enough so I can touch the bottom. Now watch carefully how I do it so you can see that I'm not so crazy."

The fox stood up, stretched, yawned, and in a single jump, launched himself over the fence out into the field. The nightingale hopped out onto the furthest branch of the bush to see better and there was the fox going around biting off one tuft of grass after the other, until he finally had a large bunch in his mouth.

"Well, I never!" cried the nightingale. "You chew grass just like a cow!"

"Not true!" replied the fox through clenched teeth as he carried the grass over to the edge of the waterhole. "I've never been so hungry that I've had to eat grass. But just watch this... I will walk backwards into the water with my tail first. Do you know the fleas don't like being in water?"

"Well, I've never thought about that. Tell me more."

"Well, as soon as the end of my tail is under water, the scoundrels biting me there will jump out, racing up my back. I keep putting more of my body under water, and as I keep walking further out into the water, the fleas rush farther and farther away from it. Do you understand?"

"It's not that complicated," said the nightingale. "But how does it end?"

"Well, that's the simple thing," said the fox. "The fleas move further and further towards my head as I keep wading into the water until finally, I have only my head above the water, and all the fleas are on it. Then I duck my head slowly under the water, with

my snout being the last thing to submerge. I keep the grass above the water, however, and the fleas jump onto it. Then I release it with all the fleas on it, and those miserable suckers drown. I jump back out of the water as flea-free as a newborn fox kit."

"Now that sounds remarkable," said the nightingale, suitably impressed. "But I'd like to see it done before I truly believe it."

"I'll show you," said the fox. "I'll do it especially for you because I don't normally like to take a bath on an empty stomach. But now I'll show you that those who say I'm the worst sneak and thief in the forest are slandering me. I'm going into the water to please you and to thank you for your lovely songs which have given me so much happiness this morning. Watch out now!"

"I'm on my guard," said the nightingale, as she nearly fell off the branch with curiosity.

The fox walked backwards slowly into the water, keeping the clump of grass in his mouth the whole time like he said he would. He moved only one step at a time and kept stopping now and again.

"Aren't you afraid?" said the nightingale.

"Not in the least," said the fox. "I've done it many times before, and I'm a good swimmer, so there is nothing to worry about. But you have to give the fleas time to collect themselves and jump forward. Otherwise, out of fright, some of them could easily and mistakenly get right into my fur, and the plan is to finish them off all at once."

Chapter 4

So, the fox continued walking slowly backwards, step by step until only his snout was showing above the water. He then dipped that right under, letting go of the grass at the same time. Moments later, he jumped up out of the water, his body twisting and spiraling as he shook off most of the water. That done, he sprang back over the fence and lay down at his place under the lilac bush.

"Now I'd like the sun to rise and shine on me, so I can get dry," he said. "I'm sleepy now, but it isn't healthy to sleep when you're wet. I imagine it will be here soon."

"I didn't see the fleas," said the nightingale.

"You can see them out there in the water on the tufts of grass," said the fox. "They are there. And if you don't want to risk that, then you can examine my fur. I'll give you anything you want if you find so much as a single critter. Good night, I can't keep my eyes open any longer."

"It's all strange," said the nightingale, but the fox did not reply.

She sat and looked at the tufts of grass bobbing in the water. She wanted to fly out to see if the fleas were there but was worried they would hop onto her. Also, she wasn't that dumb that she would fly down to where the fox was lying to look in his fur. That tricky fox wasn't going to fool her. It was nothing but a trap set to catch her.

"Red fox," she said, "I won't believe you until I see the fleas. Swim out and bring the grass to the shore again so I can see for myself if what you say is true."

The fox didn't answer. He was sleeping with his tummy moving up and down with regular, heavy breathing.

"Ha, ha," said the nightingale. "You're making out you're taking a little fox nap, but you can just stop pretending. You're not fooling me at all. I've been around in this world and know what cunning creatures you foxes are."

But still the fox didn't answer. For a few more moments, the nightingale sat looking at him and then hopped down to a lower branch, bending forward to peek at him. Yes, his eyes really were closed, and the water glistened in large drops on his fur. The nightingale was actually a caring kind of bird, and she thought it was a shame he had to lie there and catch a cold in the cool morning air. He had gone into the water for her benefit, to show her how to get rid of fleas, so she warbled fine trills which she usually did to greet the sunrise. Just as soon as the trilling was over, the sun appeared like a red ball, and its rays shone on the sleeping fox.

"Thank goodness," muttered the nightingale to herself. "He will dry up now, and I hope he's unharmed by his dunking."

She listened to his deep snores, and it seemed like he really was asleep. She did not understand whether all the fleas had drowned and had a huge desire to check things out, but she didn't dare. Then again, the fox said he slept heavily after he'd been in the water, and also that he didn't really care for the meat from nightingales. But she couldn't trust that either, naturally. Who could take a fox's word on anything? He ate her grandmother.

But it was definitely worth knowing how to take care of the fleas. That was a big problem for birds generally, remembering it was vermin did her aunt in. It would be a nuisance to go all the way under water until only her beak showed, but she supposed she could stand to do it once a year. Maybe she could do it in the middle of the summer if it meant she'd be able to be free of all those bothersome critters.

As she was thinking through all of this, the nightingale moved a little closer to the fox, hopping from branch to branch until she finally sat right above the fox's head. And still he didn't move, snoring loudly as he slept like a log. With a gulp, she hopped down to the lowest branch to see if there are any fleas, knowing if she saw even a single flea, she'd tell everyone red fox was a fake and a cheater."

She edged even closer until she could almost peer right into the still damp fur. It looked like they're all gone, and he didn't scratch himself anymore, nor shake himself a single time.

"I think I'll try it... Oh really, what can happen? I'm just going to peek, and I can get right back immedia...

Snap!

The fox lay quietly chewing on the nightingale. It didn't take two minutes to consume her from beak to tail and she was more tasty than her grandmother.

"Foolish bird!" he said, sauntering home slowly to his den

Please write a review!

Authors (and translators) love hearing from their readers.

To help other readers and children find these realistic descriptions of nature by Carl Ewald, please let the translator know what you thought about the stories in this book.

Please leave a short review on Amazon or Goodreads or your other preferred online store.

(If you are under 14, please ask a grown-up to help you).

Thank you!

P.S. Please mention what your favorite story was.

www.amazon.com
www.classicnaturestoriesforkids.com

www.ingramcontent.com/pod-product-compliance
Lightning Source LLC
Chambersburg PA
CBHW070929030426
42336CB00014BA/2601

* 9 7 8 1 7 3 5 7 2 1 6 0 6 *